# Life in its Fullness

## An Autobiography



Gods Blessing
from

Saroj & Nalesh Naicker.
Sydney Australia

naicker_n@yahoo.com.au

# Kushma Datta

The National Library of Australia Cataloguing-in-Publication:
**Life in its Fullness © Susma Datt, aka Kushma Datta 2012**
Autobiography
References
ISBN: 978-0-9874682-0-8

For information about Legal Deposit, see the website at:
http://www.nla.gov.au/legal-deposit or
contact the Legal Deposit Unit, National Library of Australia on (02) 6262 1312.



References are listed on the last page

Edited by Joyce E. James
Design and Layout by Igor Pankovic of Rainbow Print Australasia Pty Ltd,
Published and Printed in Australia by Rainbow Print Australasia Pty Ltd.
(02) 9725 2500 - sales@rainbowprinting.com.au

God takes us all on a journey through life. Some moments are pleasant and some moments we wish would never happen. I am so blessed to be a child of God, because on our different journeys, sometimes we let go of our heavenly Father because we are so hurt. God is so faithful and he never lets go of us. Although I will never understand why some things happen, I know through past experiences that God has been there for me every step of the way. I don't know what would have happened to my life or how I would have handled problems if I were not a Christian. I thank my dad and my mum for always telling me about Jesus from an early age and putting me through a Christian school so I could learn more about God. But because of the disaster of losing my dad, I can surely say that that experience brought me closer to God. I am so proud of my mum and the journey that she chose to take after losing the love of her life, best friend and husband. She has made us all look at her with pride as she grew closer to God through our family tragedy.

**Hazel Niranjan (daughter)**
Primary School Teacher
Sydney Australia

Both mum and dad have been incredible parents. Dad was a man of God - very spiritual and dedicated and a very influential man to the ones around him. He was someone I truly respected and looked up to. When dad passed away it seemed like I lost a big part of my life and that something was missing. Ever since 2000, I have seen my mother grow into such an incredible woman. She is a woman of God, with a big heart and so much love to give. The big part of my life that was missing has been fulfilled by my mum.
CONGRATS MUM, FOR A GREAT ACHIEVEMENT!

**Reginel Datta (son)**
Financial Services Administrator
Sydney Australia

Coming into a new family can be very hard and confronting but I didn't feel that way at all ,mum was very supportive and encouraging. She helped me feel comfortable and helped me settle into the family with ease. One word that describes mum best is 'Love'. She goes above and beyond for her children and always puts them before herself. She is one of a kind.

**Shazza Datta (daughter in law)**
Primary School Teacher
Sydney Australia

My Fua Kushma, has been such an encouragement to my wife, Danielle and I by demonstrating practically. what it says in the Bible in James: Chapter 2:14-17. Her generous heart and the time she gives to people make all who come into contact with her feel valued. Even with her complex health issues she continues fervently in prayer, remembering the people who have touched her and those of whom she has touched. Her ministry continues as she cares for her growing family, both her immediate family and those who are in her extended family all over the world.

**Samuel Prasad (nephew)**
High School Teacher
Sydney Australia

"Ever since we've come to Australia Aunty Kushma has been there to support us. I would like to thank you for everything you have done for me and wish you all the best for the future and for this book. Love you always, Neville N, your nephew :)"

**Neville Naicker(nephew)**
Civil/Structural Drafter
Sydney Australia

Growing up I was privileged to have known and spent time with Uncle Patrick and Aunty Kushma. Uncle was a kind-hearted and caring man who served God earnestly. Aunty is a wonderfully strong woman whose love for God is beautifully transparent. I love her dearly for the encouragement she provides to all those who surround her. Love Sarah.

**Sarah Poonan (family friend)**
Students (University)
Sydney Australia

Uncle Patrick was always a favourite of mine when I was little. I remember playing cricket with him, Reggie and Nigel. We would always have fun together. We miss him very much. Thankfully we know that we will see him in heaven!

**Paul Poonan (family friend)**
Student (University)
Sydney  Australia

I praise God for his servants Patrick and Kushma Datta. They have been and continue to be an amazing source of encouragement in both my life and in the lives of many people. I am blessed to have been a part of the journey which God has led them through. Though my journey was short with Uncle Pat, he was an inspiration. His Christian ministry through song was a motivation to begin a young women's singing group which I was privileged to be a part of. His sermons were practical and applicable to people in all walks of life. He will forever be in our hearts and his legacy lives on through Kushma Fua my (aunty) his children and grandchildren. Kush Fua has been a positive and loving influence in my life; her words have helped me rely on God's amazing love for us as His children. Her unwavering faith throughout all circumstances has made an enormous impact on my faith in the Lord Jesus. I am truly blessed to be related to an inspirational couple of God.

**Cheryl Fazio (Nee Prasad) (niece)**
Primary School Teacher
Sydney Australia

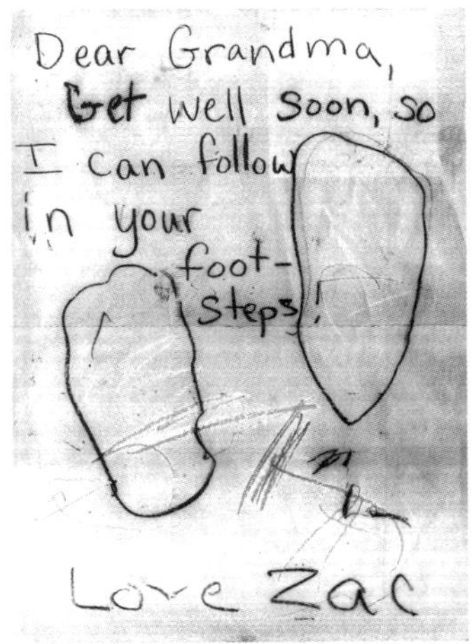

Jesus said:
**I have come in order that you might
have life - Life in all its Fullness**
John: 10:10b

# Foreword

As a pastor for over forty years, I have met some remarkable, godly people who have impacted my life. Kushma Datta is one such person. I first met Kushma following the death of her husband Patrick. Although in shock because of the suddenness of his passing and grieving her beloved, Kushma demonstrated remarkably strong faith and courage as she ministered to her three children and loved ones, as well as being available for about seven hundred people at Patrick's funeral.

She has great Christian wisdom and patience and this was evident in her role as a sole parent. Her three children love and serve the Lord Jesus Christ. They are mature, stable adults and have gained university degrees.

Kushma's ministry has been varied and wide ranging. Among other things, she was involved in the commencement of an orphanage in Myanmar (Burma). She has shared in up to 80 aged care facilities in Sydney plus Brisbane via music and personal visits, as well as taking part in all aspects of ministry in a Sydney church as a pastor's wife and later a widow. She also loves cooking and her home has always been "open house" for hospitality, fellowship and fun.

As Kushma proves God's faithfulness amidst adverse circumstances via the pages of this book, you will come to know her a little. However, you will miss the understanding in her eyes, the delight of her smile, the warmth of her greeting and the obvious love in her heart.

*1 Corinthians 1:4* tells us that **"God comforts us in all our troubles so that we can comfort those in any trouble with the comfort we ourselves have received from God"**. She endured poverty and rape in Fiji. In Australia, she experienced widowhood, sole parenting, supporting her children through health problems, a house burglary, personal pain and suffering. Kushma has certainly known "troubles". In spite of these, her life is the outworking of that verse as she brings understanding and comfort to others through her strong personal faith and trust in God.

It has been a blessing to share some of Kushma's journey over the past twelve years and a great honour to write this foreword.

**Barry Rice**
Retired Pastor
Churches of Christ
NSW, Australia.

# Commendation

*Life in its Fullness* is a captivating story of the lives of two very precious people: Patrick and Kushma. Patrick is no longer with us having finished the race, but Kushma, his dear wife has done a marvellous job in recording the journey of their faith; a faith that is founded on the Lord Jesus Christ.

Contrary to popular teachings on faith, Kushma Datta's faith is a faith that has been tested in the fires of affliction. All faith must be tested. There is no such thing as an untested faith. Faith by definition must be tested and tried. That is why this book is so special. It celebrates what God had done in the Datta family in spite of tremendous setbacks, suffering and sorrow.

Every chapter is a signpost that points to the Lord Jesus Christ—His wisdom and His love amidst the turmoil and the confusion.

*Life in its Fullness* encourages the reader to have a brand new perspective on life and its challenges.

Honesty, humour, tears and inspiration shine through Kushma's intimate account of God's amazing grace in the Datta family.

I first met Patrick and Kushma in Singapore in 1983 and over the years I have been impressed by their faithfulness in the Lord's work. But after reading the book, I see the pieces of the puzzle more clearly and I understand the Lord's ways more deeply. My faith has been truly strengthened and so will yours…if you take the time to read the book prayerfully.

My prayer is that *Life in its Fullness* will encourage you in your faith in Jesus Christ. I pray also that you will be motivated to tell and record the story of your faith, as Kushma has so ably done, as a legacy to the next generation.
May we, the readers, leave a clear set of 'faith footprints' for our family and for generations yet unborn *(Psalm 78:6)*

**Dr Jonathan James**
International Executive Director
Asia Evangelical Fellowship International

# Acknowledgements

I thank God for giving me life. This life has been difficult yet an important learning experience. My husband taught me to love "God deeply, trust and obey Him." There are no words to express my gratitude to you, the love of my life. Everything you have taught me I use for the Lord.  Your love for the children and me was so real. We miss you dearly everyday of our lives. You lived your life to the fullest everyday. I know that God had brought us together for a great purpose, to live and to serve Him only.

I acknowledge with deep gratitude the prayers, love and encouragement of family and friends.  I am especially appreciative of:

Dr Jonathan James, Pastor Barry Rice, Pastor Mathew Kuruvilla, Pastor Lyndon Ramsey and my Music Director Deborah Tin for your time and your lovely comments on the book. Thank you to all my family and friends for your lovely comments on the "Tribute" page as well as on the "Comments" pages. Your kind words of encouragement plus all your support means a lot to my family and me.

I thank God for blessing me with lovely children, Hazel & Aaron, Nigel & Shazza, Reginel and my precious grandson Zachariah. You have cared for me all the time when I was hospitalized and after. Thank you all for sticking so close to me when  was taken away from us. Nigel, you played the Father's role very well even when you were so young. Hazel, you have been a real "mother" taking care of us all, lifting our spirits. You all are the best, unique yet working together. I love you all for always being there for me. Thank you all, for every part you have played in helping me finish this project. Shaz and Nigel, thanks for all the paper work you helped me with during the editing stage. Shaz, you encouraged me every day to keep going, not to give up! Thanks darling.

Zac, thanks for entertaining me when I got really weary and exhausted.  Your part has been the most important one!

Regi, you believed in me when I didn't know that I had it in me to do this job. It is through God alone that I have come to another level of faith in Him through writing this book. Thanks for your faith in me!

My dear late mum in law has been my greatest teacher in modelling the Christian life. You were the best!  I thank each one of Patrick's siblings plus my own siblings, my lovely mum and my late dad seeing us through those very difficult days in life. Your role in my life was very important.

To all my lovely church family, thanks for your many prayers, love and support given to me. You all are my blood family (bought by Jesus' blood). Everyone of you are special to me in my journey of life. Thank you for encouragement.

My dear adopted family, Deborah, Paul, Mark and Daemion, I am really grateful that you all are in my life. Your encouragement and prayers for me daily means a lot. Without you this journey wouldn't be complete.

Mark, just when "Nani" (grandma) needed some distraction from my darkest days, you came along as a cute baby to console me. You changed my life with your love, hugs and all your lovely cute words that you said at the right time. THANK YOU darling!

Daemion, thank you for all your hugs!  All the prayers we prayed together in church, God is now answering them all. God is using all four of you in the ministry. Praise God!

I am grateful for GLO (Gospel Literature Outreach) Ministries and Lian and his family for letting us share in the dream we had for a hostel. This hostel and all the children are a wonderful testimony of God's love. They have taught me to be content in life.

Aaron, I appreciate you teaching me to use the computer. Thanks for the laptop, for taking time to teach 'the old lady new tricks' It has been worth it. You have been there always to guide me patiently when I was stuck. Without the computing skills, this book would not have been possible. You are not only my son in law but a great friend and a humble servant of the Lord.

Joyce, my sister, you are a great teacher, editor and very professional in your work. Without your help, this writing would have gone into the bin!  Thanks for the many hours you spent editing this book. Grace, you provided for my physical needs. Jonathan, your comments lift my soul. Our dad, Dr James is watching us working together for our Lord. Isn't that amazing? I really appreciate all of your love and support.

My sincere thanks go to the staff of the Rainbow Printing Press for their efficient service rendered.

To you my God, you know how much I love you! Without you I can't live.  I'm nothing without you. You God, planted the seed in my heart, then one day at a time, you taught me, drew me near to you.  This journey has been a great process in teaching me how to submit to you, love you, honour and serve you better.  Thank you my Lord God Almighty!

TO GOD BE THE GLORY!
Kushma Datta

# Contents

# Introduction

Why does God do certain things in our lives? Is it because He just likes doing them or are they for a purpose?

I believe that even before I was born He had great plans to train me. He taught me lessons in life that I would never have learnt otherwise. Right throughout, even when I didn't know God in my life, He was doing things in me. I never knew why. It all became clear when I accepted Jesus into my life. From then, I went through life with Him every step of the way.

When I struggled in life, I was angry with God He saw me and understood my pain. Psalm 139 has opened my understanding of God's intimate knowledge of me. **"He knit me together in my mother's womb and He knew how long I would live even before I was conceived. His knowledge of me is overwhelming."** He knows everything I have gone through in life, today, tomorrow and the future.

I was trained as a nurse and loved it very much. I learnt many things I never knew before. I did really well in all areas of my studies. I even assisted in the theatre with the doctors plus delivered at least twenty babies. I loved looking after patients. I worked in every ward surgical, medical, the children's ward, the nursery as well as the labour ward, as we called it then. Nothing was too difficult for me. I anticipated getting my badge as a Registered Nurse, but only a few months before I was to graduate, things changed.

Now, I see what God was doing then. One thing for sure is that my experience will never go to waste. Truly, God knows everything about me. He knew what I would need throughout my life.

After the sudden death of my husband, there was no hope at all for me. He was so very young. He worked so hard for God. I was always with him sharing in his vision for the Lord's work. I was really stuck as to how to handle life now.  What can I do? Who will teach me what is right from wrong? What about my health, my children (all in their teens) the mortgage payments that I knew nothing about? Where can I run and hide so all these problems will disappear?

It took a very long time for me to learn that no one can replace my husband. Only God can be with me all the way. He holds my right hand, saying "Fear not I am with you (Kushma)" He will make a way where there seems to be no way.  "He is the Father of the orphans and a husband to the widow." He guides me, protects me, encourages me and lifts me up from the pit of destruction. He teaches me that I will run and not grow weary and will walk and not faint. Kushma, these promises have your name in it.

It took me all this time, all the difficulties, trials plus health problems so that I can truly KNOW that God is right beside me helping me in every situation. Seeking God everyday and praising God all the way, I have come to this place in my life that He will never leave me nor forsake me. He with me, together we can do it. All things are possible with God. "I can do all things through Christ who strengthens me."  I feel the closeness with my Lord that I can ask Him anything in his name. God is ready to supply all my needs.

Not only that, He has given me beyond my expectations things I never prayed for, those things I never even dreamt of, as I know this can't be humanly possible. Things like giving me the snowfall in the midst of summer time, giving me a grandson when the doctors said "you can't have children." Things like the beautiful sunset for my son Nigel's wedding, holding off the rain till the wedding was over then bringing the biggest flood in Queensland's history.

What about the trip to Disneyland and Universal Studios? I have never ever prayed for this. This was way beyond my power to be there. He did it.  Providing lovely spouses, Aaron and Shazza for my children Hazel and Nigel, that can't be possible with me alone. What about the dream of a hostel in Myanmar and serving the under privilege children only God worked this out. Out of 46 people who trained at Regi's work only he was chosen for the job, this was a miracle only God could have performed. There are heaps of things God has blessed me in my life. The list goes on and on like in the song "Count your blessings, name them one by one, and it will surprise you what the Lord has done"

Life wasn't easy when going through the 'furnace' experience. All the pressure was too much to bear, but coming out on the other side is truly worthwhile. It's not yet finished though. As long as I live, I will have to keep fighting the battle with God on my side. As long as He is with me, teaching me, training me and being with me, I'm not afraid for my life! He is my special friend and partner. He has been faithful in the past, He will be now as well as in the future. **"Because He lives I can face tomorrow… Because I know He holds my future… And life is worth the living just because He lives"**

X

# 1   Meeting Patrick

I grew up in the countryside, where life was very different. There were eleven in our family. We were born close together in age. It must have been very difficult for my parents. They had a sugarcane farm. Their only income was from the sugarcane. They received their earnings once or twice a year.  How could they have managed with all the growing children as well as take care of the farm with money coming in only once a year?  Most of the money would go towards the payment to those my dad borrowed from all the year round. We in the family were just a number. We didn't feel the love in the family when we were growing up. Life was all work plus study. There was no leisure time, always more work like going out about a mile to fetch water, making sure we filled a 44 gallon drum every day. This was fun too as we met with our friends while getting water from the well. This job was for my elder sister and me.

Just before leaving home to do my nursing training, I met Patrick. He came to be my brother's best man. I happened to be the bridesmaid. I had never been a bridesmaid before. I didn't know what I was supposed to do. Coming from the countryside, not exposed to the 'modern world' as such, I was quite backward in many ways. I was never allowed to go out anywhere as my parents were afraid that people would abuse us.

For the wedding, it seemed the flower girls were very knowledgeable. They knew what I had to do as a bridesmaid even though the girls were so little.  I had to put the spray of flowers on Patrick's coat, this new guy in town from the 'big' city. Even though I was very shy and embarrassed, I did that but soon I had to hold his hands too, which in my culture was a "no-no". But of course I had to do everything exactly as commanded by these girls. From then on, we did lots of things together—walking side by side as well as more holding of hands. Yes, I felt butterflies in my stomach, a feeling I never experienced before. Was it love? I did feel really happy inside—that touch felt unique. What was this? I had no idea what was happening.

In fact this guy was a city guy but he looked scruffy with hair permed and dark, square glasses. His face had lots of scars from pimples. He had short pants with long socks on his very skinny legs when I first saw him. He dressed up differently for the wedding with his suit on. That day he surely looked great. The other times he looked very weird in those shorts with long socks.

Patrick's brother was supposed to be the best man for this wedding but unfortunately something happened. Patrick was just there to replace his brother. Here was this man, looking a bit older, mature but also scruffy. In my mind I thought people from the city would all look very handsome, well groomed with lovely clothes—not like us from the country side.

However, since he was there I had to make the most of the time we had together. My sisters loved his singing. We had night gatherings with lots of people at home. He was there to entertain us with his "guitar". What was this? I had never seen this instrument or heard such great music. He sang very well. Everyone loved it very much as they stayed till late at night. My sisters called me to join in the music to sing together. Some songs were from old movies that we all knew, so we sang along. Then he sang one song, looked me straight in my eye, through those black square glasses.  This is the song he sang:

"This is the night that I feel so anxious and can't go to sleep, can you keep me company until I fall asleep; Come sit right beside me till I dose off"—in our language

*"Aaj ki raat, eh kaise raat, ki mujhko needh nahi aati"*

I thought he was sending a message of his love to me. Was he really falling for me or was this just a dream? I felt good but wondered if he really felt for me or if this was the way of the city guys. Soon the wedding was all over. Everyone went back to their normal duties. Patrick had to catch a plane to go back, but I kept thinking of him a lot. Was this city guy just flirting? I told myself not to get too carried away. Maybe I would hear from him or maybe not.

My brother went on his honeymoon to Suva, the capital of Fiji, where Patrick's family lived. My brother visited them in their home. Since Patrick had given me his address, I thought I would send him a thank you letter. I wrote: "Brother Patrick, thank you for coming over to Labasa (this is my country town) staying here, entertaining us with such beautiful songs. We all loved the music." He sent a letter back saying "it was a pleasure being there.  I was so nervous of your dad though, he looked straight into my eye that scared me to death". My dad was always drunk. At that stage he wasn't a Christian. He also knew the motives of guys, and sure enough he kept a watchful eye on us girls. He wouldn't say much, but his actions spoke a lot.

When my brother returned from his honeymoon to the city, one day I heard him talking about some very important matters with mum. We "young" children were never allowed to hear when two adults were talking. I hid behind the curtain to hear what he had to say. The news was that Patrick's mum Mrs Masih was very concerned about her very sick son. He had a heart problem. He was getting older. She was keen to find a good girl for him to get married. She needed someone who could really take care of him. She was worried that he might never get married with his heart condition. Who would want to get married to a sick person? My brother explained to mum, that he was the person who was here for the wedding. His mum had been praying all his life that he could have a surgery to fix this problem. Nothing had happened.  But right then they wanted to start looking for someone decent for him. When I heard this I was shocked, stunned and very emotional, I felt very sorry for Patrick. How difficult it must be for him to live this life.  As a very young Christian myself I told God: "I don't know what you want for me in my future. I felt sad for this person. If you want, please allow me to take care of him. I'll be happy to love him and care for his sickness." This was my little secret prayer to God. My brother and mum were the "only ones" who knew of his problems. Wasn't that smart of me to listen?

In the meantime, I had applied to go to the Nursing Training School. This happened to be on the same island where Patrick lived. Fortunately, it was about eight hours away by bus to their home. There was no way we would be able to see each other, even if we fell in love, which didn't happen immediately anyway. I received my acceptance letter from the Nursing School. My brother made all the arrangements for me to travel with dad via Suva where Patrick lived.  We had to take a bus trip to my nursing school. It happened that our first stop was at Patrick's house. I didn't know anyone there except him. My brother asked them to help us out as we were new to this city, which they very kindly did. We spent a few nights at their place.

This house I noticed was very different. It was like a hostel, a free hostel  People from many places lived in this home. Mrs Masih also adopted three young children even when she was old and grey. She had a lovely smile always serving people as they came to her house. She cooked and fed everyone even if she didn't have much in the home. She was always doing good things for all. At 6pm every night she got everyone together for prayer. I joined in this prayer session. She prayed for many people. She even prayed for me going to nursing school. I felt happy to have someone care to pray for me. My dad even though he wasn't a Christian, she prayed for him. I saw lots of love in this home.  I really wanted a home like this plus I definitely wanted to be like Mrs Masih.

While I was helping Mrs Masih in the kitchen one day, she suddenly asked me a question.

"Would you like to get married to my son?"  "What a proposal!"

 I was shocked, but I just smiled and turned away. I don't think Pat was aware of the proposal mum had made to me that day. Patrick came home after work, said a quick hello then went into his room. He came back to the kitchen later. He had boxer shorts on, I was stunned. What on earth is he wearing, I thought? It looked so bad I just couldn't believe my eyes. We didn't talk much at all, except he asked as to what I was going to study in nursing.

My dad and I left for a very long journey to Sigatoka. This is where my eldest sister Kamlesh lived with her husband. It was a very long twelve hour trip. I thought I would die on the mountain tops and valleys. The road was very rough.  We were both very exhausted but were happy to see my sister and my brother-in-law who was a school teacher. We spent a few days there before we all left for my nursing school.

**Patrick's health and family**

Patrick was born with an extra muscle in his heart. It was very difficult for Mr and Mrs Masih to see their son suffer. While their other children were healthy, they concentrated on Pat's health since he had difficulty in breathing. As he grew up, his problem became worse but his family took good care of him. His older brother helped Pat carry his school bags as he wasn't even able to do that. He couldn't participate in athletics or sports of any kind. He felt bad that he wasn't a normal person. He had to go to hospital every month to get an injection to help him breathe easier.  He got very tired of this as time went by. Throughout all the problems in his life, Mum always prayed. She believed that only God can do miracles. At school, Pat did very well in his studies right throughout his schooling days. His work was outstanding. Pat always felt he must work hard in the academic side as he couldn't do sports.

At one stage, the heart specialist put him in hospital so he could carry out a simple catheter test to check his heart out and where the problem was. After the test was done, Pat couldn't sleep that night. He felt something was happening to his right foot, he called the nurse, they came to check but then went away telling him to go back to sleep. He called for help throughout the night as his foot felt really heavy. Again the nurses gave him injection to put him to sleep but this lasted for only a few minutes. He continued getting up throughout the night because of the pain. When his specialist came over in the morning, he saw Pat's leg had no blood supply all night, he was horrified. He quickly took him to theatre and operated on him to see where this clot was moving around in his body. The doctor opened the groin area. He found a big clot which, if not operated on, would have killed him that day. The specialist was very angry with the hospital staff. We praise God that again this wasn't any accident but something God allowed in Patrick's life. And we believe that even in this it seems God saved him from dying that day.

As if this wasn't bad enough, there was more to come. The doctor who operated on him, took the clot out and sewed up the area in his groin. All was going well. Patrick was in hospital for a few days. While the operation site was still very raw, the nurses took the stitches out and sent him home. He told them the pain was unbearable, but they merely responded: "Who is the doctor you or me?" When Pat got home, the operation site opened, he was bleeding profusely. His brother Mike had to take him back to hospital to admit him again. Pat was there for a very long time. Mike always took good care of Patrick, even though it took six long weeks. Mike would go and be with him at hospital besides all other things he had to do for his family. Patrick has always admired him and appreciated all his kindness. He always felt that Mike had taken his father's role and took care of all the siblings.  Their own dad died of a heart attack when they were very young. Mike sacrificed his own education to put food on the table for the family who was already struggling.  We owe Mike a lot for the loving kindness he showed to all his younger siblings.

Many years went by and in June of 1976 Patrick was given a chance to go to New Zealand for his heart operation. Praise God, there were no mishaps this time. Four days after his surgery he was able to walk around the hospital. He felt so light in his body for the first time in twenty-six years. What a relief! He went into surgery with great confidence and with no fear. Patrick was very excited that God had given him such a beautiful verse the morning of the surgery: **Psalm 118:17: "I shall not die, but live, and declare the works of the Lord."** His health was excellent for the next twenty-two years—no pain, no tablets or injections. It was all over. He loved his life, his Lord and served Him with gratitude in his heart. I have never seen a man so dedicated in serving the Lord with a humble heart and a deep passion for people. I am so thankful to God our Saviour that Pat came close to death many times yet no one could take his life away until it was his time to go. I know he is in Heaven with his maker the Lord.

Why did God bring all these things into his life?  Was it for training or building his character? If it wasn't God in control here, then who else was? God was building his character in one way and preparing me in another. As he went through so many health problems, I believe this was the reason God took me into nursing to gain all the knowledge I could to support Patrick in his work. God knew how to put two people together in marriage. For a city and a country person from two different islands and two entirely different backgrounds to be compatible is amazing. Only God in His wisdom could do a miracle like this. Praise God for who He is—the all knowing God.

# 2  My Life in the Country before I found Jesus

We in our family were very religious. We went to worship Hindu gods. This was a routine thing for us. Young girls from the village were there to compete as to who can do better in these temple duties.  We went there to meet our school friends as we were not allowed to go to their homes. Often we ended up fighting over petty things. I was always frustrated in my life. We kept telling lies to get higher in this temple as leaders of our Hindu club. This went on for many years. The things that were happening around me seemed all right on the surface, but behind our backs people were so very nasty. In my heart there was no peace.  All of us in my family were the same. Our behaviour was rotten with hatred, anger, jealousy, bitterness and the rest. I give you one example: (On the day of my wedding, two of my brothers were going to kill each other with a machete) What a lovely memory! That's how bad our lives were.

My eldest brother became a Christian through some friends. My brother shared in the Happy hours which we looked forward to every week. There were lots of stories we didn't know. In one of those meetings my brother chose few of us to go to a camp. He virtually forced me to go. This was far away, also "in a plane," that was too overwhelming. This would be my first plane ride and first time away from home (over the local seas).What's happening? Before that, I had not known anything about the world. (My brother had another motive but he was only witnessing for Christ – well done brother!) I was excited to leave home—that would truly be freedom. That would be my first plane ride too. My dear brother paid for me to go. It was there that I heard the Gospel for the first time. That day I gave my heart and life to Christ and accepted Jesus as my Saviour. This was the first time I knew that someone loved me very much and was prepared to die for me. I was a sinner in God's Holy presence. Jesus had died on the cross but rose on the third day and is now our Risen Saviour.

The fact that I could go to Heaven because Christ had paid the price for me was too overwhelming. I remember that day very well, it was the 17th of May, 1974. A good friend Naomi showed me all these verses from the Bible. I gave my all to Jesus. Praise God that He first loved me and chose me to be His child! I discovered in

**John 1:12  If I received Him, I would be called the daughter of God! Thank God for opening my eyes—I needed a Saviour who cared for me.**

For the first time I talked to God, this living God. This is what we called "prayer" I told Jesus "Thank you Jesus, you loved me so much to die for my sins. I am a very sinful person. I have done wrong things in my life. I want to live for you, doing things that will please you.  I want you to forgive all my sins and clean my heart. Come into my heart and live in me. Thank you, Lord Jesus you give me Eternal life in Heaven. I want you to guide me in all I do. Thank you that you have made me your child now. I love you in Jesus name Amen"

When I got back home from this camp I kept praying for myself. This was a very new thing for me but I challenged this God. I used to have a very foul mouth—swearing was our life. I told God about my rotten behaviour and asked Him "if you really are the True and Living God, take this swearing habit away this very week" Oh! How I praise God that truly He is a risen Saviour! He did it, although it wasn't until weeks later I realized I hadn't sworn for all that time. What a victory in Christ I had—halleluiah!

Just as well, my eldest brother became a Christian first.  He had a "say" in the family matters. He could reach out to others. Things would be different if I became a Christian as I would not be allowed to go out to talk to others about the Lord. Our culture limits us girls from many things. Well, God knew all this in advance and He did a perfect job in getting all our family to know Jesus.

After my conversion, one by one all my family came to know Jesus, and I praise God for this. Eleven of us all gave our hearts to God. It took about thirteen years for all to make their decisions but they all did. My dear mum, even though she doesn't read or write, is on fire for God. I'm grateful she is a committed Christian. My dad's conversion really became the "talk of the town."

 My dad was an alcoholic from a very young age—every day he came home with a bottle of alcohol. At the age of seventy-five, he gave his life to Christ. It was a great miracle that dad had no desire for drinking after that. Could this be possible? Well, it was possible—it was right there in front of my eyes. What I saw in this man was dedication. He sat down reading the Bible day in and day out. Praise God he trusted the Lord. He died at the age of 87 years, never drinking but living for God.

"What has gone wrong?" his drinking friends asked him. "Maybe you're mentally ill. All these years we've been together. How can you let us down?"

They kept begging him to go back to the pub, which had been his second home for over sixty years. Praise God he witnessed to these friends. They saw the true happiness in my dad's new life. Only with God was this possible. As we all came to Christ, we prayed for our friends and neighbours to follow the true and living God.

When I became stronger in my faith, I became more confident in talking and sharing with other people. God gave me more energy, also the power of the Holy Spirit to do His job, so talking became no problem. Then every time I went back home to the other island, I encouraged my other family members to speak up and communicate with those who are quiet and shy. Thank God that today, even though all my family come from a countryside background, with God's great love and the confidence He gives us, He uses us even to this day. All my brothers and sisters are serving our great Saviour, in whatever part of the world God has put us! What a blessing to have a lovely family!

My eldest brother Shiu and I went into full time service for our Lord in the same year. We are still serving Him up to this day. It has been more than thirty-five years, yet it feels like we have covered very little ground in these years. There is no job like this—we may not be the richest people, but we are rich in Christ, in His mercy. He has provided all our needs.

There was so much that happened in my family. I am writing this now not because I hate what happened, but so we can all learn lessons from it. Our family was very big. Mum and dad had nine of their own children and three adopted children from my dad's previous marriage. Mum was very young when she got married.  She took care of my step-brother and two step-sisters as well. Our family was like a factory just producing children—almost every year, someone was born. In this situation, how could anyone show individual attention? We all grew up with this background, and I personally feel I wasn't given love and care. Even touching, hugging and encouraging were foreign to me.

I felt so good when my mum took out head lice from my head because that was the only time she touched me. I always looked forward to this and for me, it didn't happen often enough! Surely many country people went through this, so I also speak for them. We all were just a number and never felt special, individual love and care. We never seemed to have any time for play or relax.  Being poor was the worst thing for me!

Even when we went to school, we had to borrow ten cents from our neighbours. People got tired of lending us money, as it happened so often. My poor mum was told off by our neighbours and received terrible abuse. We really were very poor and in great debt all the time. Dad was always drunk. We had a dreadful life, with no purpose. It seemed like we were failures in every area of our lives.

God had this part of our lives under control too. If we as a family hadn't gone through all this hardship, I don't think we would have seen the miracles of God that came later. As our family started their journey in the Christian life, one by one accepted Christ into their lives. Then we saw many changes happening in our home as well. Even with the little income that we earned, God blessed it and we were never without food, water and clothing—and lots of repair jobs were done in our family home too. We realized it could only be God doing these amazing things in our home. Like in **Matthew 6:33, "seeking God first and all other things will be added to you."** We put God first in our lives and God did the rest. Our neighbours were surprised to see that there were great things happening to us. We had many missionaries coming to stay and help build God's work.  Amazingly, God was now using our family to witness to our neighbours. After many years of praying and witnessing, when I went to my dad's funeral a few years ago, I discovered many of our village people had given their lives to Christ and started a church in the village. This was such a blessing to see. Praise God for answered prayers!

I think in the countryside people love, respect and care for each other very much. We all addressed our neighbours and friends respectfully by calling them 'aunty', 'uncle', 'brothers' and 'sisters'. We all loved one another— but there was another side of life, people were not aware of.

The worst experience of my life was when I went to keep one of my neighbours company. Her husband had gone away for a few days with his job and she was lonely. My parents never allowed us girls to go anywhere at night. But this time, the lady begged mum to send one of us girls to stay over with her. When I went over that night, I saw that this lady had hidden a guy behind the door in her house. I had the shock of my life, as to what he was doing there. I was very young (about nine years old) and didn't know anything about sex and periods, as our family never openly talked about such things. We were never taught about these things even in school.  We trusted everyone. I called these people "brother" and "sister in law."  Anyway, that night this big fat guy raped me there in front of this woman. I was horrified, scared and didn't know what to do. I struggled so I could run away but couldn't. He was too big and strong. I was so scared—I didn't know how to respond to this woman who had betrayed me. I fainted and had no knowledge of what this guy had done. This lady should have saved me, as I trusted her. When I woke up in the middle of the night I saw this person in my bed.  My heart was thumping. I wanted to run and hide, but there was no place to hide and it was so dark. I had knots in my tummy and felt so sick—that scary night I went through was the night that changed my life forever.

In the morning, I went home so ashamed, frightened and bleeding for the first time. How could I tell anyone at home? If I told mum, she would get really angry. She never wanted us girls going out at night anyway. If I told my older sister, she would then let all the neighbour's young girls know about it and they all would laugh at me. We didn't have a good relationship—we always fought, insulted each other and let each other down. We lived with no love in our home so I couldn't imagine getting any sympathy from anyone. I hated myself for going over there. I had never had a period before, now I was bleeding and was even more worried what would happen to me. I locked this in my heart. I didn't know why I was bleeding. What if this man did something that started the bleeding? I was constantly living in fear— how could a man be so evil? My whole life was such a mess. Every month when I had my period, I thought it was the result of that rape. Never could I trust anyone enough to tell them what happened to me that night.

In high school, many years later, I learnt that all girls have periods and why this happens. Still, I went through my life with this grief in my heart. This aspect of our country life people will never find out but I know many girls, like me suffer in silence for years.

When I met Patrick, we talked about marriage, I told him one day about this ordeal I went through at such a very young age. For the first time in my life I could trust a guy. How relieved I was that I could share this burden I had carried for years with someone who could understand my pain. Thank God, Patrick helped me throughout, understanding me and teaching me to let go of this problem. I started to feel secure around guys. I was so happy Pat was a Christian person whom I could trust with all my heart. He was always there to protect me and guard me with his life. Now, I praise God for His angels surrounding me and that I can trust my loving Saviour and my God to keep an eye on me every day of my life.

Yes, life in the country was not as you might know it. There were so many problems that we couldn't even talk about.  There were no counsellors who could help. I have learnt so much through this evil experience and empathy for every rape victim.  Every time I see something about rape victims on the news, I think of my own ordeal. It is only with God's help that I have now been able to let go of it – God has indeed helped me through this big problem I faced in my life.

God knew about every experience I went through, but sometimes I wonder why God didn't protect me in this situation. I know God chose me before I was born, to serve Him so how come He let me go through such a painful ordeal in my life? Did God make a mistake? Did He forget me then? I don't think so. I do believe that every experience in life is for training our hearts, minds and building our character to be more like Christ.

At the back of my mind was one question? Why did he do such a terrible act? I carried this burden for all these years. Why had this man done such a rotten thing? I could not forgive him. I prayed that he will have daughters born to him and that they will be raped one day. I needed to know why he had done such a crime. 40 years later, I confronted him by phone.  It was shocking to hear what he had to say. He told me "he couldn't even remember doing such a crime". What did this mean? Did he rape other girls as well, that he couldn't remember? It was shocking for me to know what he was like. Oh what evil people live in this world! I asked my God to help me let go and forget the past. I prayed to God to give me that power of forgiveness to let go and forgive this man just like Christ forgave us all our sins on that cruel cross of Calvary.

That day, I truly felt a big burden lift off my shoulder. Only through God's grace and forgiveness could I forgive this sinful man. I felt so light in my mind, my spirit and I thank God that through His love, I could take this big step.  I was 50 years old.  I prayed God would use me in ways I had never imagined.

Memories of what happened lingered on as I looked at that house every time I went back home.  The pain returned over and over again as I continued to suffer in silence.  Can you imagine this: One day mum invited "this" visitor to our home.  Since he came from oversees, they were "very important" people. Since mum didn't know any of these things, she ordered me to give him a cup of tea. I was shivering, tense and so tight, I couldn't ever think of seeing him ever again. Now I had to take mum's order to give him a cup of tea. You will never understand the pain in my heart. I quickly put the cup, not even looking at him and ran away to the toilet.  What a torture this was for me!

I was really happy to leave this place to go away for Nursing School. Being so young in my faith, I didn't even know much of the Bible and forgiveness.

**Days in Nursing School**

When I arrived at the nursing school, I felt really sad. I knew I wouldn't have any of my family around, just new people from all over the place. I cried as I said goodbye to my lovely family. I was praying God would show me some good girls I could have in my life. They were all new and we all got on well together for a while. Emma (Emily Taylor) was the best of my friends.  She was a great Fijian girl I got to know. We shared lots in common. We had fun and fellowship together all the days there. She joined me to my church sometimes. We both loved the food as well as the company of these lovely members of our church. This was a time I will never forget.  As I think back now, we were like the Christians in the book of Acts. We all ate together and had wonderful fellowship and prayer. I was a "baby in Christ." They all built my faith. The fact that the meetings were in the Fijian language didn't matter to me. I enjoyed listening and was able to follow the communion service. The Holy Spirit was my teacher, showing me great things as I followed them in the Fijian language. These years of love and encouragement from my church folks were truly such a blessing to me. Many of my friends were able to see real Christians in action.

At the hospital, we also had a Christian fellowship.  It was very different to what I knew about Christianity. People prayed one moment, the next moment they fought in anger for petty things, had hatred, jealousy and gossiping. This really bothered me. When I was in the dormitory with other nurses I would just learn more from God's word. This was better than getting involved in gossiping with others. I had a lot of learning to do anyway. This was the time to do it. Many times, I had to stand up for my Lord. Lots of nurse's behaviour was really bad.  I just prayed much for these girls. I asked God to give me wisdom, as I didn't want to be part of their rotten jokes and filthy language. As I prayed, God helped me, in addition He used me for His work there.

Girls in the beginning said to me: "You Holy, Holy person". They insulted me but I just let it go many times. Soon they saw something in me, one by one they all came to me for help. I told them I can only pray. God is the only one who will help. Many girls came over for prayer. God worked, He answered my prayers for them.

I'm so thankful that God was working his miracles in my life plus using me for others too. It was really great to work and serve the Lord even as young Christian. I'm happy that the rest of my stay got better. They respected me, so did the people in the leadership and the Matron. She suggested to the girls in trouble to go and talk to Kushma. I feel that this was the reason God took me away from everyone from my family. This place was a training ground for me. I built a deep spiritual relationship with God, in studying God's word plus standing up for Him.

All throughout my nursing days, Patrick kept in touch with me. Both of us were able to send letters to each other. Later stage as we got closer, we talked a lot on the phone.  A few times he came over with his youth group from his church. They all loved Patrick and teased him about falling in love. They knew that he was one person who will never fall for girls but "what's happened now Patrick?"

They made up a song for him and sang "across Ba bridge there is no more sorrow, across Ba bridge there's no more pain, the sun will shine across that river, and you'll never be unhappy again." "Ba" is the name of the place I was doing my nursing training. There surely was a long bridge they had to cross to come to see me.  Whenever they arrived from the 8 hour trip from Suva, they lived with one of the church elders. They were lovely people who took great care of the group. Patrick would come to see me with all his group members for one hour or two. Then all of us went to meetings in church. Whenever they did come over they had two reasons; first to see me but the other was to preach and teach in the church. When we got to know each other really well then Patrick asked if I was serious in this relationship. Of course I was. Wasn't that my secret prayer?

Patrick mentioned to me that when we did get married we would serve God together. That was the desire of his heart. He asked me how I would feel about this. I was very happy even though I didn't know much about the work. I was happy to learn and serve God together after we were married. The work would involve visiting people. Patrick needed me to be with him in the ministry. I prayed about this situation. Knowing that nursing requires night, evening shift work etc, I then decided to finish my course without graduation.  I mentioned the future plans to the Matron and she was sad I was leaving.  When she heard both of us were planning to serve God as pastors and teachers she was very excited. I left nursing with the blessing of such a wonderful Matron. She wrote the most beautiful letter mentioning how effective I was in being a mentor to the girls. I felt a bit sad to say goodbye but God was preparing me for greater service. I wanted to follow what God had in mind for me.

I have never regretted this calling of God. God has blessed my husband and me in this most wonderful job. A job which had a high calling: to serve youth, children's and later the seniors. Our greatest blessing has been to see many people coming to know the love of Jesus and giving their lives to Christ. What more do we need?

As a young Christian still, I really wanted to study at a Bible College. This would equip me for my service for the Lord. God in the right time opened the door for me to be at this Bible School to study and prepare for my future ministry. I knew I will be in full-time service for the Lord. I didn't have much knowledge of Scriptures except what I studied myself. These studies were for 10 weeks. That meant the timing was perfect.  When I finished here, it would be time for our wedding. This place trained me for many practical aspects of my life in ministry as well.

Kushma's Siblings and Mum at Dad's funeral 2007
Front row: Rajen, Roshni, mum, Nalesh
Back row: Shiu, Kamlesh, Saroj, Kushma, Sunil, Suresh

Patrick and Kushma at Mount Panorama, 1998

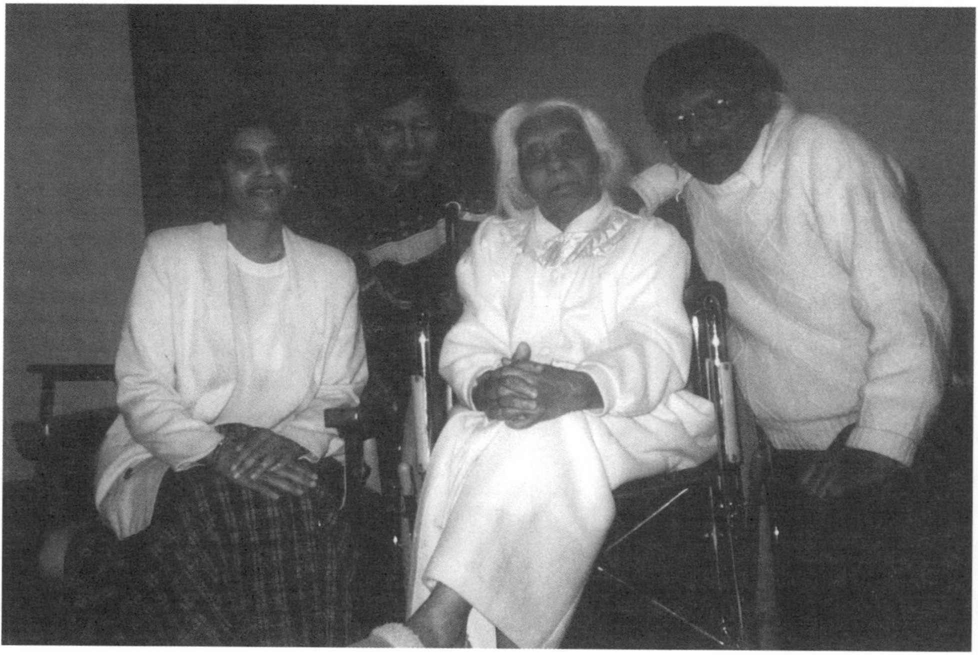

Patrick's Siblings
Susie, Silas, mum, Patrick (Absent: Michael, Ruth)

# 3  God's Calling and Early Ministry

This Bible School training was timely. In addition to studying I learnt many of life's lessons at the Bible School in Fiji. The Principal was Mr Foster Crane.  His lectures were great. As a young Christian I learnt many spiritual lessons from these studies. I loved learning to cook new things. Mrs Crane was a very good cook. She was a very godly woman. She always had time for all of us. I stayed at this college for ten weeks but learnt a lifetime of lessons. I'm grateful to God for allowing this to happen. I know God was training me for my future ministry. I learnt about organizing things in catering, cooking, preparation of food, menus, doing the roster and all the shopping that was involved. God knew I would be involved in future schools camps as well as other ministry so this was a great preparation time for me.

I'm forever grateful for Mrs Crane's loving kindness in teaching me many things in life. My mum in law always talked about Mrs Crane's kindness to her. When my mum in law as a child was rejected by her own relatives, Mrs Crane a white missionary showed mum an Indian, love when she was sick, massaging her head. It was never seen before and was mind blowing. Surely this was Christ love in action. This really brought my mum in law to love this God as well. Then over 40 years later, I came to see the same; Mrs Crane's love in action. Praise God for their godly, sacrificial lives at this Camp Site in Deuba.

## Our Wedding

After Patrick's open heart surgery in June of 1976, we got married in December. Patrick and his friends flew over to our Island. My family members were not all Christians. This was the first Christian wedding in my home and my village. Our whole village enjoyed seeing something new and different.  We had a crowd of more than seven hundred. They all were very surprised at everything that took place. Not only that, we had a feast for three days and nights. It was really an expensive business.  After a week we had a reception in Suva, where Patrick had all his family and friends come to celebrate our wedding.

I loved the passion Patrick had for the Lord. I learnt many lessons in my own life through his dedication and love for God. He would get up in the morning, with his guitar singing "Lord help me work another mile just one more time, I'm tired of working all alone" or songs like "Just a closer walk with thee" or "Central's never busy always on the line, you can talk to Jesus almost any time". He was a great believer of having joy and peace in his deepest soul everyday of his live. Truly, I married such a gracious, godly person.

We lived together for these eighteen years. I have great memories of this time with mum and my lovely sister-in-law, Ruth. We have been good friends for the last 38 years.

While serving God, mum was our biggest supporter. It was the desire of her heart that at least one of her children would be a missionary or a pastor one day. We found out later in life when she mentioned this to us, but definitely this God called us into ministry.  Thus mum's prayer was answered. How great is our God! He knows every step we take.

**Early Ministry**

Patrick and I decided to leave our careers to serve the Lord. Some people in our own family became very angry as to why we had made such a stupid mistake in our lives. We knew that God would guide us to whatever His plans were. We knew we were taking a step of faith. This would be our work and service for the Lord. He would provide our needs as He provided for Abraham in Genesis. I really appreciate the faith of my husband as well as my mum in law.

The Principal of the Gospel High School approached Patrick at the accounting department of the Government Building in Fiji. Patrick was asked if he could take a position as the Head of the Scripture Department. At this stage he was doing very well in accounting, getting promotions, getting up the ladder in his work. He was paid very well. He inquired of the Lord and surely his heart was for serving God. He started this job at the Gospel Schools in 1974.

When we got married I joined Patrick in teaching Scripture at the Gospel Primary School. I loved serving the Lord, teaching God's word to children, their parents and sharing about Christ in Happy Hour clubs. Children came to know God in their lives. This was the most satisfying thing in life. Just to know that these kids were now on their way to Heaven filled our hearts with joy that no money can bring. Many lives were changed in high school as well as in the primary school. People from Hindu background as well as many nominal Christians really knew what it was to believe in God. Amazing things happened. We believe God had put us both in the right place as we continued in the ministry in schools.

We took many young people who were serious in wanting to serve God, taught them and trained them in Christian living. Many came from non-Christian backgrounds. They didn't have much support and encouragement at homes. We brought them under our "wings" so they could see and learn with all of us working together for our Lord. We took them with us to many outreach meetings, teaching them how to evangelize, do visiting and sharing their faith. Praise God many of these young ones are now great leaders, elders of churches and even Pastors here in Australia, Fiji, Canada, New Zealand and many parts of the world.

Life wasn't easy as we continued in this work, as Satan also had been at work while we served God. There would be times when we didn't have much money in hand, but we needed things. We prayed continually. We knew God had plans. He would provide but sometimes He tested us till quite late when we really needed to pay for something urgent. In the last minute someone would come over to visit us and give us just the exact amount we needed. God has been very real in many experiences we have had and today I can tell you that every experience has been worth it. If it wasn't that way, I would never learn to trust God the way I do now. He truly is a faithful God who answers prayers. One thing I kept learning from Patrick and his mum was that we must pray, pray and pray. It is good to be praying for every little thing as God listens to those who cry out to Him. I praise God, he reigns every situation in our lives teaching us lessons from it. The more God provided, the more we trusted in Him and his power. This brought us closer to each other and God. We kept on trusting His wonderful power day by day. We both prayed with my mum in law. Every day she kept praying for her children far and wide.

After four years of our marriage, God blessed us with a daughter Hazel. She was beautiful. God definitely blessed her. God gave her a beautiful voice to sing. Dad and Hazel sang for the Lord all the time until dad was taken away. She does other ministry rather than singing now. When she was three years old, we had to decide whether to take her to Singapore or leave her so we could concentrate on studies we will be involved in. After much prayer, we knew it was good for her to stay back so we really could study abroad.

When God called us to go to Singapore to study for three months, we had lots of difficulties. We didn't have bags, shoes even clothes. I went to get myself some clothes from the second hand shop. I got four nice dresses for fifty cents each. They all were beautiful, I was so grateful for them. Not everyone was happy about us going away, as some of my own rich family even insulted me for using second hand clothes. That didn't deter us—we just kept doing what God called us to do. It hurt me but nevertheless I continued to forgive people and let go of whatever they may say. What God was doing in my life was just teaching me to be patient. God provided our fares to Singapore, our boarding, food and all our stay was looked after. How amazing was this! God was saying to me: "Let go and you will see all the blessings I have in store for you". What a great reward when we found out that all our expenses were paid. We just needed to take our bags and go.

Dr G D James, the founder of the Asian Evangelical Fellowship, was behind us going to study God's Word in Singapore. The course was on Evangelism and Missions. This study was for three months. He arranged for us to go to visit Madras (Chennai) to preach in remote areas for a few weeks, preaching and teaching in churches there.

Dr James was like a father to my husband and me. He and his wife Rose daily prayed for our work, studies, our children and our future. Many years ago when we first met him in Fiji while doing Evangelistic work in our country, till the time of his death, he showed us great love and care. I am truly amazed at what a godly father he was to us. We were very blessed to have him in our lives as a mentor and a friend too. We knew him for over twenty-five years. He definitely enriched our lives all the way. He encouraged us, taught us plus helped us financially many times. I am so indebted to him. I always prayed that one day my children will be like his children, everyone serving God powerfully in different parts of the world. Praise God for wonderful godly parents!

When we were in Singapore, Dr James took us to many different churches. He introduced us as his own children. We felt great in a strange land we had a dad who loved and cared for us both. Paul did the same with Timothy and others so did our dad. Our stay in this country was a great experience. The believers in Singapore were so genuine and strong in their faith. This really encouraged me to live a better life for Christ. Every day I was learning new things, seeing new places, tasting new food, meeting  new people, visiting churches, learning new cultures and doing lots more things.

One Sunday after lunch, for instance, a friend took both of us to her home. When we arrived there, it was just like "Heaven had opened its doors and windows and given us so many blessings that there was no room to store them all." What I mean is, she just opened her wardrobe, took out dress after dress, heaps of skirts, tops, handbags, belts, pieces of jewellery and many more things for me. Truly I was in awe! I didn't know God was preparing this day for me. Remember, I only had four dresses from the second hand shop in Fiji. Look what God had in store for me! I couldn't believe it. For a while, I thought this girl must be crazy or sick. I wondered what was wrong with her. She virtually emptied out her big wardrobe full of clothes. These clothes were beautiful, new, clean and neat. The amazing thing was they all fitted me perfectly.

Why would God allow this? When we faithfully serve Him, He surprises us. He is no man's debtor. He knew we had left our jobs to serve Him. He knew how we were serving Him with all our hearts, even though all wasn't easy. This is why I said "He opened the doors and windows of Heaven and showered us with all these blessings." Thank you, our 'Jehovah Jireh' the Provider, who gives all good things to his children. What a blessing!

After finishing our studies, we went to India to preach and teach in different parts of Madras. We travelled all night and arrived at 5.00am.  From 6.00 – 9.00am, Patrick preached in a hall full of people. They were really hungry for God's word. They would sit cross legged and take in everything that was said. Every sermon had to be three hours long. I felt for Patrick. He had to preach twice a day for ten days but could not sleep in the train when we travelled during the night.  By the end of our trip, Patrick was sick with a sore throat losing his voice altogether.

It was time for our return to Singapore from Madras. We had travelled all over the countryside. While busy with the work, we forgot to reconfirm our return tickets.

"Sorry, there's no room left for you as you didn't reconfirm your tickets," they told us when we arrived at the airport.

"Please do something for us as we have a connecting flight from Singapore to Australia too," we begged them.

They got busy and we got praying. "Please God, only you alone can help. These people don't seem to be interested to help. God, you know our situation. Please help"

When the counter got less busy, we went again and asked, "What can you do for us?"

"We'll see, can you wait please?"

A little later, the man called us and told us to catch a bus to the aircraft. I wanted to ask what was happening. In such a rush, he was in no mood to talk. We just followed his instructions. As we got to the plane, the stewards called us into the first class seating area.

"Is this a mistake or what?" we wondered. "Hope they don't tell us to move later."

I didn't feel comfortable, not yet!  They must be wrong. When the plane took off, we both held our hands and prayed. "God, how awesome are you?" You keep surprising us with so many of your blessings. Here was Patrick, so sick, tired and exhausted after the tiring time we had for 3 and half weeks. I can say "God was doing things behind our back."

We gave thanks to God, praising Him with all our hearts. We even thought we didn't deserve it, yet God wants to give us precious gifts to enjoy here on earth. Yes, there is reward for us in Heaven.  I also believe God rewards us here on earth as I have experienced so many of His rewards and blessings here.

As we travelled on the plane, enjoying every piece of luxury, we rested and Pat, at last could sleep a little with the comfort of the first class seats.

We looked at the date of our travel. Suddenly we realized that "today is our 7th wedding anniversary" "Oh my God, no wonder you created all the fuss at the airport, LORD - for us to travel in style!" What an experience!

As we kept travelling, I wished we didn't have to stop over in Australia, with Pat's health really bad now. It would be better we were at our own home. Both of us thought.

We wanted to see our daughter, while she was enjoying her time with my mum and sisters. It was really a long time.  She was only three years old. We were imagining being home and the excitement of seeing our family, but specially our daughter.

We continued our long journey. I spoke to the air hostess on board. She went and fixed something on the computer and came back to tell us; we were fine to fly to Fiji when we landed in Australia. Oh my! Was this real or what? Oh what a feeling that was! All our imagination came to reality. My dear husband was so excited that he started feeling better immediately. He was "over the moon", in fact. We went on dreaming about how we would soon see our lovely daughter and our family too.

Again God's faithfulness to us was way beyond anything we imagined. **Ephesians 3:20 says: 'He is able to do exceedingly abundantly more than we think or imagine.'** What a powerful God we have! Great is our God and greatly to be praised. We had a truly wonderful trip home to Fiji. I thank God for things that were given to us by many friends. What a reward! Even when we got to our country and needed to get a local plane to my mum's place, God even had that ready for us so we could be with our daughter on the same day. What a lot of travelling that was, but it was all worth it.

Together we gave so little of our time for the Lord's work in Singapore and India, but God gave more to us in return. How can we ever forget His kindness and love in our lives? Every day was a blessing in one way or another. The blessings we received were nothing that we deserved, but in His wisdom He showed us that even what man can't do, God is able to do with His mighty power.

He knows every step we take. When we take it for Him, that step is such a rewarding experience for us. If we don't do it for Him, we are the ones who forfeit his blessings. Thus we regret and don't have peace in our lives. I am so grateful that we both chose to serve our risen Saviour. He gave His all for me; I want to give my life to serve Him even now when I'm not well. He is able to use me, if I am available to Him.

**Jeremiah 1:5 says:**

**I knew you before I formed you in your mother's womb. Before you were born I set you apart.**

I thank God that He brought us together. We were married in 1976. We started serving the Lord full time straight away. God had been preparing us in many ways in ministry and in our own lives as well. When I look back I see how little I knew then and how much God has taught me so far.  God has blessed many children in schools, camps and in many different meetings. Many gave their lives to Christ. Amazingly, we even took teams of up to twenty young people to different parts of Fiji doing evangelism and training. It was really hard work. Patrick and I had to be very organized to do this. In everything we did, we prayed and prayed. God had His miraculous hand upon our trips and the people. We had great blessings in this as our team members learnt to live with one another working together in groups. Many students were encouraged to live for God better as they went back to their homes.

Out of those trips that we did often we found out there were so many talented young people whom God was going to use in the future. Today is that future and praise God for his wonderful blessings that these young ones, now much older and mature are here in Sydney and many parts of Australia. Some are really dedicated in serving God and building the body of Christ even when they have secular work. Many are doing God's work in other countries as well. Some are pastors, elders, doctors, teachers or lecturers. They all are serving the Lord faithfully. One of these families I visited often in their homes (in Fiji) while they were strong Hindu then, today this person has pioneered  two churches and has built one orphanage in India. It's great to see all the fruits coming forth as we continue to sow more seeds now to the next generation. What a blessing it is to serve our God!

Right throughout my life on many occasions I was offered many good jobs with "better pay". It felt like it was a test for me. As we struggled financially, many times I went to the interviews. I did not feel at peace at all. I questioned my motive, and knew I was letting my God down by taking this job. I let go of these jobs and continued with the best job that God had chosen for me. The exhilarating thing in this job is winning souls for His kingdom.

After having three young children times were tough. The cost of living became higher every day. We needed to pay school fees and all the other expenses that go with schooling. This is one thing we never did throughout our ministry, is to ask for support from anyone. For the first time Patrick asked a few families if they could help us out through these difficult days. Some wonderful people happily contributed and helped us out. Others told us that we were "parasites" that we are depending on them to take care of us. "Why don't you go and work at a petrol station, Patrick?  "I thought your God would send you money, a house and a car from Heaven!" I felt ashamed to call them my family. My heart was torn to pieces when I heard this.  Yes, we depended on God for meeting our financial needs.  God only used human beings to help provide all these needs.

That day my heart cried out: "God what have we done wrong?" "I wish I was not born to hear these words" I didn't know what to do. I hated myself and what I just heard.

"Have we really made a mistake, serving the Lord?" I asked Patrick. "Why has God allowed us to hear these words from our families? I can't go back to serve the Lord—I feel very hurt in my heart."

18

That whole week I kept praying, asking God what is next?  Show us the way, tell us clearly if we have made a mistake in serving you! That week, two of our church members invited us to their place. Even though we didn't feel like getting together with people after what had happened, Patrick forced us all to go and spend time with these lovely people. That night God said to us: "Keep serving the Lord. Don't look back!" We were so excited God did a miracle in our lives. These two couples gave us a lovely car as a gift. I was so excited! Why? I wondered who told these people about all we went through. No one did except God!

How amazing is my God who knew what we went through and how our hearts were aching. No "God didn't throw us a car from Heaven" but gently gave it to our family using godly brothers and sisters. Perfect timing!  If you say there is no God, then who was this? Was this a coincidence?  No definitely not. I know my Saviour lives and He cares for our needs. God was sad when we felt hurt and were crying out to Him. He saw all that happened that day.

Even today I feel God has truly blessed me more than all other family members. This is not of any good thing I have done. Only by His grace and mercy, He called and I answered to this great "calling."  It's not because I want to boast but to glorify my God through whom all things have been possible. He is no man's debtor. It is very exciting to tell of the wonders He has done in my children's life and my own life. Praise God who owns the cattle on a thousand hills! We know that being a servant of God is not easy task.  There are many days of happiness and joy to see the fruit of our labour. Then comes trials and difficulties we never think we'll have to go through. Why would God let us go through these times? In this difficult world there will be many problems. When we choose to honour and serve God, the reward is incredible as you have seen in my own journey.

Patrick's extended family
Front row: Reginel, Nigel, Michael (Patrick's brother)
Back row: Satish (family friend), Ruth (Patrick's sister),
Hazel (our daughter), Eunice Masih (Patrick's mum),
Kushma, Patrick

*Cheryl's (Kushma's niece) Wedding 2006*
*All of Kushma's siblings and their children*

# 4  Falling out of God's Will (1987)

Patrick stayed at the Gospel Schools for more than twenty-one years while I did seventeen years of service, including all the "Compassion" work both of us did. When the children were born, I had to be home to take care of them for a while. Many years went by and we continued to trust God and serve Him in the churches and in the Gospel Schools. God continued to bring many young people to Christ through this ministry.

Making decisions in life was not easy, and I felt that sometimes we went on our own way not knowing what we were doing was right or wrong. One time, Pat told me he felt so much that God was calling us to a new ministry in New Zealand.

"Why do you want to leave Fiji and the work there?" I asked him.

"Maybe it's time for a change," he told me.

I didn't feel too comfortable, but I thought maybe God is speaking to him and not me.

As he investigated more about the job in New Zealand, he said 'yes' to the people at the Baptist Church in Auckland, so we could start some Hindi outreach work there. They told him all our fares would be paid and all our household items will be shipped at their expense. Patrick had to give our travel dates to them and all would be taken care of. As I started packing and selling things from home, my heart wasn't fully at peace.

"Are you sure we are doing the right thing moving to New Zealand?" I asked Pat.

"Yes, we need a change—and this is the right time," he said.

The political situation in our country was really bad. After the coup we had, lots of Indian people migrated because of all the difficulties they faced. Unfortunately, it also affected our churches. Pat was still feeling that we must go and this was a good opening for the future of our children. Time passed, and all the big household items were packed by the shipping company and taken to the wharf. We sold all the things we couldn't take over, such as the beds, wardrobes and dressing table. We had great farewells in both my school and Pat's school and the churches we worked in. Everyone was very sad to see us go but they didn't want to be in God's way if He was calling us.

Our flights were just a few days away. I got really sick with my back problem—the same problem I had for years now. Whenever I had this problem, I would be in bed for days and months. My mum would come over from the other island to take care of me and do virtually everything for me. When Pat called my mum to come over this time, she couldn't as she had another grandchild to take care of in her home. Pat begged her to come, but she definitely couldn't. He even wanted my mum to come over with us to help us in New Zealand. Pat was also depending on me for Hindi work. He didn't study Hindi in school so it was all up to me and my health. Then he realized if I was sick in bed and not able to help him when we started this new work there, it will be a disaster. Even for driving, he needed me as he couldn't drive much as a result of the surgery that affected his right leg. How could we handle this work if I was so sick? Nothing was working out. I was very concerned.

"Do you think we're going away with the right motive?" I asked Pat. "Is there anything wrong with the choice we've made?"

I wanted to know what was in his heart. Only then did he mention to me that he was trying to run away because of all the church politics. Many church people weren't behaving like Christians and it hurt him. What could we do now? Could we still go? It was too late. We had all our farewells and received gifts from many places—it would be embarrassing to go and tell our people what had happened. Besides, we had sold all our things. We didn't have anything left in the home. We asked God to forgive us for our mistake. We continued to pray for wisdom as to how to "break the news" to people now. "God, only you can speak to the people concerned. Please help us now to do the right thing" It was like Jonah in the Bible running away, what should we do? It was better to be in God's will and feel embarrassed now, than to go out to serve God in New Zealand without any blessings.

We went to tell the school staff first. They were so excited and happy to hear we were staying back.

"We couldn't see you both going away," they told us.

Whoever we told about our staying back, the reaction was great and we felt very accepted. The funny thing was all our household items that had been sent to the wharf to be shipped to New Zealand had been packed by the workers for many days. What could we do about that? Pat had to tell them we were no longer going. They were shocked to hear that we changed our mind and were not going. They didn't know how much to charge us as this had never happened before. Eventually, they decided they would let it go. How wonderful we didn't have to pay for anything.  All the hard work these few men had done for days was wasted! Praise God that even when we had made a stupid mistake, here was God still helping us. His love never ends, even when we are not faithfully listening to Him—our great God is truly amazing. God knows everything in our hearts and there is nothing we can hide from Him. This was a great test for us to go through, and we were so close to a disaster in our lives, but God saved us. *One good thing we learnt from this was that when God opens a door, no one can close it, when He closes the door, no one can open it.* This is what we went through. God didn't want us to leave, somehow He made us stay. This time it was my health problem that opened our eyes. I'm so thankful it happened that way.

God blessed our church ministry in bringing many more people to Christ that same year. Also nineteen people were baptized, and their ages ranged from ten years to eighty years. Among them was a policeman, a school teacher, a taxi driver and his family and many students from our school. That school teacher died a few months later, but we definitely will see her in Heaven. How wonderful it was that she came to accept Christ as her personal Lord!

**Getting out of God's Will (the second time (1997)**

Patrick graduated from the Emmaus Bible. While at College, we helped many struggling churches through our ministry.  GLO (Gospel Literature Outreach) Ministries was in our mind for very long time. God opened the door for us to serve with them. We really enjoyed serving with godly believers we met daily. We were reaching out to the Indian community in Blacktown area. (My health got worse by the day.)

The children were then in High school  and they needed finance to keep up with the payments. We were stuck many times. I remember those days so well when dear brother Lian with Patrick spent hours in praying as I lay in bed sick unable to get up.  In the heat of the day both of them went to different churches to see if anyone could finance us so we could continue with GLO work. For a few weeks this was their job. Many of the churches were already committed to supporting other missionaries oversees so it was difficult for them to help us as well.

We were also helping Belmore Church of Christ in ministry from time to time. This was my brother's church.  Whenever we visited my brother's family, they used Pat in teaching God's word in their church.   They begged us to help them in the ministry permanently.  They needed a Minister to lead the church for some years. Pat was one who in his mind was strong in changing churches.  He was a Brethren, he was going to die a Brethren.

Patrick told me one day that we need to pack up as we will be leaving for Fiji. He felt in his heart to move back to Gospel School.  On the other hand I didn't feel that.  I said to him how about we pray for another week and see what God has in store for us. Every day we sat down to ask God for His guidance and wisdom. "Only then we will decide what's next for us." I told him.

In the meantime, my arthritis was getting worse. Someone suggested that I see a Rheumatologist.  My appointment with this doctor was on a Thursday. When I saw him, he told me "this arthritis is really bad. The treatment is long term, maybe a year or even twenty years. I need you to come and see me every month, take the tablets I give you, do a blood test every month as I need to see the progress from this." Amazingly, I'm still on this treatment and it has been fifteen years now. I'm much better in health, arthritis is under control. I'm living a happy life but only with many tablets and injection.

This result was of God and nothing else. Why was God using the doctors to keep us here in this country? He can do anything or use any circumstances so that we can keep doing His Will. After I explained to my husband everything the doctor had told me, there was no doubt in his life that God had answered our prayers.

Before my doctor's appointment even my brother Rajen from Belmore kept encouraging him to take this position. One of our disciples from Fiji, (living in Sydney) also noticed all that was going on in our lives. He has been our helper, supporting us in the past, a very close friend and he has always been there for us throughout our stay at Emmaus. He told Pat "why are you running ahead of God? Don't you know that in Heaven we won't have all this divisions, Baptist, Gospel or Church of Christ?  It's all God's work.  As long as the doctrines are right you should take the job" Nothing could change his mind. "Only God got through to him, straight to the point," Thank you Lord!

Thank God we obeyed the Lord, as we saw great blessings in the years that followed. This was the first paid work for us throughout our 23 years in service for the Lord. I thank God for using Patrick in such wonderful ways in this Church.  He wrote in his journal "God has kept the best job for last in my life" Surely great and mighty things happened as we served God in this church at Belmore.

Running away from God's call like Jonah has consequences.  We have surely experienced this before. Being obedient to God however, brings joy and satisfaction. Going through all this was very painful. We had a very heavy heart, but once we changed our minds, our hearts felt at peace. That's exactly where I want to be in my life, feeling that peace in every thing I do. I want to do His will in my life every day, every month, every year of my life.

*Patrick and Kushma, 1999*

# 5  Challenges of City Life

Coming from a rural background I'm happy to say that God definitely gave me a passionate heart for people.  We would give our lives for our people, that's how much we loved and cared for everyone. Later it gave me a good start in my work with the children in School, friends as well as parents. We as young children were not even allowed to talk to adults when growing up but now I was an adult. It may seem unbelievable, but when I got married to Pat, I didn't know how to talk to anyone in church. Pat would tell me to talk to people and I would shy away.

"What do I talk about with people I don't know?" I asked him one day.

"Ask them how they are, talk about the weather and then about their hobbies," he said.
It took me a while to start conversation with people, but now there's no stopping. I talk too much— that's what my husband said and now my children say the same!

God put Patrick and me together for a reason. He was a great teacher and preacher. Anytime we needed to go out to visit, he was totally different. He needed me to be there to start a conversation with a stranger or a new parent. He knew I could do this better. He always wanted me by his side whenever this sort of situation came up. I believe God knew our weaknesses and strengths. We always worked together. I wanted to be his shadow, following him and doing little things wherever he needed me, but God's plan was totally different.

Pat's family was Christian.  They were all believers and very dedicated, serving God faithfully.  Everyone loved God.  Every Saturday was our "Open Air Outreach." We all went to help in the city.  With all those who were living with us, they couldn't run away from this responsibility.  Some were singers, others just talked to people as they passed by. Michael, Pat's elder brother was our speaker.  His voice was amazing. He could sing as well as preach.  Many heard the Word preached. Only eternity will tell who gave their lives to Christ in those meetings.

My whole family loved Michael's preaching and teaching. They all looked up to him. He was the first Indian preacher in our country. We loved seeing him advertised in the local papers with a lovely picture of him. Truly my life was affected from his teaching. This whole family had great love for God and love among all those who stayed with us in that family home. (Remember my own family background was really shocking.)  Theirs was a lovely family that I admired.

In the city life I also had to learn to be very open when we talked, they always talked every little detail to their family. We could never talk like them in my home. I was learning fast. Another thing was when taking girls out for all the camps I had to be ready to take them for swimming.  I had never exposed my body to people but now I had to wear swimming togs, I found it very difficult.  Even when we were baptized in the river I wore a dress to cover myself. This was a real pain but that's how it had to be.

Country life was so easy going in a sense that we didn't have to always rush everywhere. We couldn't go out at night. We didn't have electricity. We knew we had to get gallons of water, take the clothes to the river to wash and then do dishes at home.  In the city we had to get home from school then rush to meetings one after another. I felt life was too busy for me in the beginning. At my place at the end of the day, we all would get together, sit around, enjoy our family dinner then go to sleep around 8pm. Now all was changed we kept going until late at night.

I believe that even before I was born, God had chosen me. Just as we see in **Jeremiah 1:4, 'He set us apart'** to reach out to our own people in Fiji, and later in Australia. **"All the days ordained for me were written in your book even before one of them came to be."**

 How great is our God, to know me so intimately and still choose me to serve Him, the King of Kings! Whatever I went through even as a non-believer, all was known to God. All the poverty, all the pain and every experience was not in vain. This was God's way of preparing me.

I have learnt how to talk and share with people after some "initial hiccups."  God has been very gracious, loving and patient with me His servant. My life is a journey of learning from others. In this journey, many difficulties and struggles came our way. I learnt to count all the blessings, naming them one by one and it has surely surprised me what my God has done in my life.

*Kushma in Disneyland, 2008*

# 6   The Trip of a Lifetime

My mum was in Canada with my sister for about six months. It was time for her to leave for Fiji and she couldn't travel alone. As all my siblings were busy, I made myself available to assist her back to Fiji.  This was the only reason I was in Canada.  While I was there I met up with all my friends and families.  It was lovely to be with my husband's younger brother and family.  This was my first trip to Canada.  I had a great time with all my families.  There were some things I was scared to face though. This neighbour who had raped me, had now migrated to Canada with his family and were good friends with my family.

Before I went to Canada I mentioned the rape to my own family at home.  Regi, my youngest one was really furious. He decided to come to Canada with me.  He told me that he was going to kill the person. After a lot of discussion, he understood that I will have to do this on my own and deal with the problem myself. That's what I did. As I said before I spoke to this person on the phone. He said "I don't even remember" Can anyone rape a young girl and forget this in a hurry? I could not even believe what he said. This was very hard but I decided that I will forgive him as Christ forgave me. Now, I had made a decision to let go. As for me, my burdens were lifted and I felt free in my heart.

As I mentioned before, never could I share my rape ordeal with anyone, (not even my family members) My family had a good relationship with this person all these years. This was very painful for me to know. "If only I could tell everyone what he had done!" After 41 years when I opened up to all of them in Canada, it was a different story. They were all shocked when they heard the news. They were really very sympathetic.

As for me, I was carrying all this burden for so long. Now that I confronted him, I thank God that I have been able to let go and forgive him just as Christ has forgiven me and died on the cross. Only because of what God has done in my life that I had that resurrected power available to do this forgiveness.  Without God I couldn't have done this.

The very next day, God revealed to me, "I'll reward you with greater blessings in life to replace all the years that the locusts had destroyed." One thing I never prayed for was to visit all these beautiful places.  I never even dreamt of going to Disneyland and Universal Studios. I could not envisage ever being there. Financially it was impossible — NOT WITH GOD! He opened the door for my son Regi, cousin, Amanda, my sister in law, Rose and I to take this trip. This amazing trip was a gift from someone very dear to my family and me. I dare not mention his name. I couldn't believe such a thing would ever happen. It was God using such a blessed Christian to bless us. My mind was overwhelmed and my heart bursting with joy. What was so impossible in my mind was now happening in my life and so fast. Was this real? We visited every corner in the Disneyland and Universal Studios. I was privileged to see the "Golden Gate Bridge", "Salt Lake City" as well as many other fantastic tourist attractions in the United States.

At the Theme Parks, we checked in the hotel for four days.  We took every tour in the Disneyland, taking every type of pictures with all the characters, like Simpsons, Shrek, Cinderella, Jasmine and many other characters. Regi and Amanda went berserk, went on all the rides they could. Rose and I sipped our coffee and rested a while.  The four of us went on some rides that weren't too scary. For four long days, we were in another world, enjoying every area of the Disneyland and Universal studios.  We took lots more pictures when we got to the Universal studios.  We saw where all the movies were made, like "Monster Inc," "Shrek," "Pirates of the Caribbean," "Bug's life," "Cars," "The Mummy," "Jurassic Park," "Hulk," "Incredibles," and the making of movies like "Fast and Furious," "Desperate Housewives," "Finding Nemo," "Police Academy," just to name a few.

Do you think God is alive? Does He watch over us and give us a reward? GOD JUST DID THAT!  He gave back to me much more than what I had lost. Oh yes, I believe this was all God and no one else. He used someone very special and godly to bless us this holiday. We had the time of our lives! All four of us enjoyed every moment of the days. God is truly such an awesome God. I am so thankful to Him—I love and adore Him.

While in Canada, one more very interesting thing happened that only God could have brought about. Before I left for Canada, my son Nigel said to me, "Unfortunately mum, you won't be able to see the snow when you are in Canada." He was there during December and January and loved experiencing a white Christmas and playing in snow. One summer day (it was April/May 2008), suddenly we heard the following report on the news: "We have never had snow at this time of the year, but something's happened! There's snow all over the houses, on the mountains and everywhere!" As I looked at this snow, I told Silas what Nigel had said. God knew the desire in my heart to see real snow. Silas got Rose and me into his car as we drove to Frazer University. This place was covered in snow. We rugged ourselves up in our coats and beanies and went out to play in it. I had to get photos as evidence of God's goodness to me. What is impossible with God? Hasn't He created the whole universe?  All things are possible with our great God. What an amazing sight this was for me! What was more amazing, God holds all seasons in His hands.  He made the sun, moon and stars. He alone could do this mighty miracle, even out of season. God is able to do exceeding abundantly more than we ask or imagine. Praise Him for the beauty of God's creation!

Why am I writing this?  He does great things in our lives. I needed to surrender my whole life to my God. Forgiveness is really hard. For 40 long years I chose not to forgive this evil sin of rape.  When I chose at last to forgive, my heart was free of a big burden. It was a heavy burden to carry all these years. When I didn't forgive, I was the one suffering. Deeper and deeper my pain got worse. Even when God said **"Cast your burden to me I will take care of them." 1Peter 5:7**. I chose NOT to do that, I wanted answers. Now I choose to obey God studying his word daily and filling my heart with His promises. Now I claim His words on my life as I do my daily chores. Even with little things such as praying for a parking space at the right spot, close to the shops (with my weak leg problem). I even pray for the sun to shine for one hour so my clothes can dry on the line—and God surely has answered these little prayers. I am amazed when I go shopping God takes me to the places where there are specials on just the items that I need. Is this incredible or what?  It's all about trusting by faith this living God, moment by moment.

I am no different from anyone else—I am a sinner, forgiven by God's grace and mercy. I surrender my life into His care every day and I feel good and very peaceful. I can pray about anything, whether it's big or little and He has been faithful in answering these prayers of mine. God also knows when to say "yes" and when to say "no." You can see also that sometimes I didn't even pray yet God gave these trips to Canada, Hollywood in America. I love these "BONUS blessings."

God does everything in our lives for a great purpose. We have to except "his will" in our lives. Even when times are tough we can keep going and say like **Paul "I can do all things through Christ who strengthens me."**

*On top of the Sydney Harbour Bridge, 2007*
*What a feat!*
*Kushma, second from the right, front row*
*Nigel, second from right, back row*
*Reginel, thrid from right, back row*

Universal Studios, 2007,
Kushma between the jaws

San Fransisco, 2008,
Kushma and cousin Neelum

# 7  Health and Family

When we got married, one thing we decided was to enjoy each other for a while before thinking of children. Patrick's theory was when the kids came, He will be going out on his own to minister.  He always wanted me by his side.

After four years, we were very excited when I found out I was pregnant. My face was very dark and I was really big. I thought this was normal. I had a great doctor who cared for me throughout my pregnancy. I always thought there will be many problems during this time.  I had a normal pregnancy and delivered baby Hazel within 4 hours, then I had complications.

I had a great friend who took care of me throughout my pregnancy. I was still in school teaching Scripture. My dear friend made some very special food daily and would wait for me to have lunch with her.  She lived next to my school and would stand near her door waiting for me. Mrs Latiff was a great woman of God. She was excited that the baby was coming, she sewed many things in preparation for the arrival. I loved the way she prayed with me and for me. All her children were very close to me. All of them were truly excited that Pat and I, young full-time workers were having our first baby.

Just three days before my baby was born, my dear friend Mrs Latiff had a brain haemorrhage and passed away. It was the biggest shock in my life. Both Patrick and I respected her like our own mother. She always encouraged us in the ministry. We loved her very much. Now everything had changed.

The funeral was planned for the Tuesday. I told Pat "don't stop me, whatever happens I am not missing the funeral service." That would be the way of paying my last respects to her. Tuesday morning came and I had some bad stomach pains. I never had pain like this before.

"What on earth has gone wrong?" I asked Patrick. In spite of the pain I got ready for the funeral. This pain went on and on, getting worse.

We waited for a while then realized this might be the contractions that the doctor had been talking about. This could be it. Patrick said we should get to the hospital in case the baby was coming. With a heavy heart and painful contraction I was in hospital in no time.

 The baby couldn't wait. I was in hospital by 9.30 and my doctor arrived. I was in the labour ward, thinking of my dear friend. As my pain became worse and worse, the doctor asked Patrick to come in as the baby was coming. At 1.30pm, a beautiful little girl, Hazel, was born to Patrick and me. How proud I was to know my baby was healthy—and she was such a cute little girl.

As for Pat, soon after the baby came, he ran to the crib to check if everything was okay. He was so worried that the baby might have a very weak leg or even a heart problem like him. There was no way he wanted this baby to have any of his problems. As he checked the baby, the doctor assured him she was perfect and healthy.   What a great relief it was for him!

Something strange happened that day when the baby arrived at 1.30. My dear friend Mrs Latiff was laid to rest in her grave at the exact time Hazel was born. Is this coincidence? This is a precious way to remember my dear friend every year on Hazel's birthday?  I was so much in awe as to how our God knew the friendship we had. Forever He made it possible to remember her. I really valued all her children who cared for me. They all loved us and encouraged us both in our faith.

We praise God for the great gift of Hazel to our family. She grew up with all different nationalities.  All the people in our church looked after her as their own baby. We were very blessed to have these wonderful people in our lives.

Hazel grew up beautiful and with a great singing talent. All her life she was spoilt by many friends with lots of gifts. Since we could not afford things, every gift she received meant a great deal to us as full-time workers. Mr and Mrs Daya Nand were full-time workers in Fiji for many years and had migrated to New Zealand. They knew the many difficulties we had as workers in Fiji. Together with all her children they enabled us to travel over to New Zealand— their lovely daughter Gwen paid our fares. The whole family collected a room full of things for Hazel, from baby size to about six years of age. They had toys, sheets and baby clothes of all different types—everything. What a great surprise!  God used wonderful people like them to supply our needs. We are forever indebted to them for their generosity, the love and care given. God really blessed us as we continued to bring up our "one and only daughter" that is what Patrick boastfully called her.

When we went to India we were so thankful to God that Hazel was not with us. The pollution, the people on the streets, the dirt, the food we had to eat, the places we went to everyday as well as night travelling was too much for both of us to bear.

One day when we were feeling very homesick, I told my friends about my three year old daughter Hazel who was back in Fiji with her grandparents. They were very surprised that I had left her behind. They asked me "do you know what Hazel means?  Hazel means "whom God looks after" They told us. I was astonished. Thank God that's what He was doing in Fiji, "looking after her" while we were on our mission trip.

Surely God had been looking after her all her life from the moment she was born till the time when we arrived in Australia and later, as we went through the toughest things in our lives. We all grew better and stronger when we were left without my husband and their father. We depended on him always for all the decisions and choices we could and couldn't make.  Now we had to think ourselves and pray to our Heavenly Father's help. Where else could we go anyway?  Life was very tough for all my growing children.

I have been grateful that Hazel was much older than the boys. She has been there by my side to help me when I got stuck many times in decision making in certain situations. I called her my "right hand man." even though she is a lady. Just a few days before Patrick passed away, he took her for enrolment in the university. She found it very hard to concentrate at the university.  She asked me to go and sit in class with her. Later she found some very good friends. They could all work at our home studying together and doing some group assignments.

Dad was a great influence as far as study was concerned. He wanted all the children to do well at school. He always told them that they must study hard to achieve their goals. Even for Haze, when she told her dad she wanted to be a hairdresser, he made sure she still had a good career. He suggested she do hair dressing after she graduated. She wanted to quit University when she found it difficult. I would stay awake with her helping her finish her presentation or assignments. Praise God! Through prayers and with God's great help, she graduated as a teacher.  Now she is a wonderful teacher.

One prayer God didn't answer for 23 years of my life. This surely was tough but God had a reason.

The back problem started the day Hazel was born. I had very high blood pressure straight after the delivery. The doctors gave me an injection and put me to sleep.  I lay unconscious in one position for many hours. When I got up that day I had that back problem. I continued to do things in a normal way, not realizing it was making my back worse. I did heavy lifting, as I didn't want my husband doing that since his heart wasn't too strong. When I did huge amounts of cooking at many camps and weddings, lifting all the big pots and pans, it was not helpful. As the years went by, this back problem became worse. Many times my mum would fly to my place and take care of me, as I was like a baby. I couldn't get up, shower or walk any steps because the pain was so excruciating. My mum was there for me every time Patrick asked her to come. I'm so grateful to my lovely mum for doing everything for me, taking care of me, cooking and feeding all of us.

I suffered back and spine problems since 1980 and as I prayed about this, God kept taking care of me. I continued to endure this pain for twenty-three years before I was finally operated on. Surely God put me in bed to rest my body. I went to hospitals in Fiji.  I left my family for three months back while I got treatment in New Zealand. I went to see many chiropractors, had acupuncture done as well, but nothing helped. Of course, I really needed to rest my body too, but as a pastor's job requires much, we always felt on call full time. The people we worked with couldn't understand that we as leaders also needed our rest.

They all depended on us to keep going, until my back gave way many times. Then alone I could rest in bed completely for a few weeks and slowly I would recover. This time was for me, a time to "BE still and know that He is God." I wanted that time with God alone. I needed to get refreshed with His Word and learn more things that I needed to share with people. Even through this time of sickness, people came over to see me. When they visited me, while I was sick - I would share how God has been so good in teaching me lessons through my illness. God used my back problem to make me rest.

We were trying to have a second baby for a few years. I couldn't have any more children. We went to doctors for help but nothing happened.  After five years I conceived Nigel. In our family, we always wanted to know who could possibly have a baby boy. Our Masih/ Datta families in Fiji tended to have only girls. I remember one of our families mentioning to Patrick, "There's no way you'll have a boy. We all have girls so you will have a second girl too." That day I opened the Bible to **Psalm 127:4 (GNTUK) "Sons are a heritage from the Lord; children a reward from Him."** I felt so relieved to see that verse and continued to pray. Was God going to bless us with the first son in our family? What a blessing this would be!
Patrick was so honoured to see our first boy born. It was very exciting having a boy who would take his father's name to the next generation. Nigel is the name we gave him. Why? Well, we always had hurricanes and storms in Fiji.

Cyclone Nigel had just passed when Nigel was born, so it sounded very nice to me. Later when we came to Australia, we realized it means being alone or lonely. I felt really bad, but we can't change it and it still sounds beautiful to me. I'm very grateful God blessed us with Nigel.

Straight after delivering Nigel, I went into the public hospital as my back problem had become worse. I had lots of complications before having Nigel. I was in the maternity ward for a month before he was born. When I went into the public hospital, my mum cared for Nigel. Then mum was called by my sister who was having her first baby. Poor mum took my baby, looked after my sister and her baby as well. What a life she had! The funny thing was that since Nigel was only a few weeks older, he had my sister's breast milk. Their little baby wouldn't feed much—so look how God provided for my baby! "Don't tell anyone!"

I spent about six weeks in hospital. My eldest sister had all the sick ones at her place in Ba. She, together with mum cared for us all. When I was discharged, my dear brother Rajen travelled 6 hours, taking me to where my mum and my baby were. I admire all my families as they have been there helping me in time of my need. Unfortunately Patrick couldn't be there with us as he was working.

Just imagine this! I'm recovering from my back problem. Very few times Pat was able to visit me the sick lady. Suddenly this "Bengali" had done something I got pregnant again. "No it can't be!" I thought. It was soon confirmed by a test that I had a surprise package in my womb.

"Patrick, what are you doing? Don't you see how my sister is suffering?" said my brother.

When God chooses to give, no one can stop; so here was our precious Reg. Everything went smoothly throughout my pregnancy. For a few months I thought even my back problem was gone. For my labour, Hazel took four hours, Nigel two hours but with Regi, there was express "service" no waiting. Within an hour he was born, beautiful and very fair. There are no mistakes with God, even when we felt he was a surprise. All things are known to God. He knitted Regi in my womb. What a blessing he is to me now! God has great plans for his future. God's promise says:

**Jeremiah 29:11**

**I know the plans I have for you, declares the Lord, plans to prosper you and not to harm you; plans to give you hope and a future… (NIV)**

Growing up Regi only wanted his milk bottle nothing else mattered to him. He was content in all other things. He was a great baby playing with Nigel and other kids happily.

As for Nigel, it was a different story. As a baby he was big and fat. He was always hungry and was such a big eater. He was always busy, very playful but he took good care of Regi. We would always see these two adventurous children keeping busy. They were good friends and Hazel was the mother, always disciplining them with very strict standards. She acted like a teacher from very young age and thus the punishment for the boys was harsh. Hazel loves art and is very creative and she is very good in the way she trains her own son Zac as she did with her brothers.

34

Regi was only thirteen when he lost his dad. Nigel was fourteen, one year older. This was very difficult for both of them, as in their teen years, both boys needed their father. This time in their lives was as challenging for them as it was for me. The only thing I could do, with God's help, was pray with them and for them every day. What else could I do? Who could I talk to about everyday difficulties? I had to run to God and beg Him to do something to help. Sometimes I also talked to Patrick. "You are there, sitting in God's presence, so close to Him," I would say. "Tell God I really need help. Please help!" This is really weird, but many times the answer came even through this. Whenever I needed help, I tried my best to call on my God in every way possible. Even for the children, going through these challenges and difficulties, was for a purpose. God has been building their character the same way I feel God was dealing with me.

Nigel had difficulties with his studies. He was more of a practical person l ke me—no reading just playing. He did not do very well in school.  Patrick had to keep pushing him all the time. Every time he was told to do some school work, he would do it for two minutes and then be gone. He was a very good artist. In high school he did one picture that was displayed in school for years. Both the boys loved sports as well in school. They both love music as this was dad's hobby. Regi plays the guitar. Nigel plays the guitar and drums in his church.

 One surprising thing happened when Pat passed away, Nigel got very serious about studies. He worked very hard and scored good grades throughout his school and university studies. Now I thank God my children can stand on their own feet at the ages of twenty-six, twenty-seven and thirty-two.

One dinner time just before he passed away, Pat told Nigel "If I'm not around Nigel, you being the elder son have to take care of the family.  Use all my sermon files to preach.  You will be taking the job of a dad in the home" Nigel has taken that role since he was 14 years old. Thanks Nigel!

Belmore Church, International Bible Study Group, 1998

Fellowship with the my Pakistani "sons", at Windsor 1999

# 8  Abrupt Ending

The year 2000 was a great year that we were all looking forward to. Our family knew we were hosting the Olympic Games in Sydney for the first time. We were going to celebrate my husband's birthday and it was to be a big celebration since it was his 50th birthday. He normally didn't like parties—especially if they were for him. This time, however, he agreed to have a big one—but only if we allowed him to make it the most unusual party.
"What do you want to do?" my daughter asked.

"I'm going to play with mud, so let me do that," he told us.

"Whatever!" we said. "At least we will all have a big party."

Anyway, whenever we went driving past Olympic Park, we saw how the buildings were going up and all the huge stadiums were under construction. Also, many roads were being built, all in preparation for these Olympic Games. One day as we drove past Pat said to Pradeep, (one of our disciples from Fiji) "I wonder if I will see these Olympic Games?" "I don't think you are going back to Fiji so God willing you'll still be here to see this, Patrick," he commented.

Once Patrick began work in Belmore Church, we took our break during school holidays. This allowed us to travel together with our children. We visited many places in the Mountains. Patrick was able to spend a lot of time with the children during this time. Some of these times we spend in a special house that was rented out at a very affordable price to ministers and pastors.  We thank God for this lovely place in Katoomba in the Blue Mountains.  All our family loved this home and went travelling to other nearby tourist attractions.

In January  2000, we went to Katoomba in the Blue Mountains again. We stayed at the same holiday house. Previously, we had gone together to the ninety degree Scenic Railway, Leura Gardens, Railway Museum, Three Sisters Waterfall and many other places. We even went further to the Jenolan Caves.

This day as we drove from Belmore we sang songs all the way for fun. We all had to find a song with one letter someone chose. It was funny—Pat had all the songs sorted out and was definitely the winner. Some of his songs were 'What a friend we have in Jesus', 'Have thine own way, Lord', 'I am weak but thou art strong' and also 'Lord, I'm coming home'. We all had our turn at choosing songs, some Christian songs and others just secular songs.

It didn't take us long before we were in the mountains. By mistake, we went to a crematorium. I thought it was a garden but when I drove in, I discovered it was for those who had died. Anyway it looked so clean with lots of flowers, so Pat and I had a cup of tea, but the kids were too cold to get out of the car.

When we arrived at the holiday place, it was not ready yet as the cleaner was late. She asked us a favour if we could come back to the house in one hour. We then went to Wentworth Falls. We all enjoyed it there in the sun and played games. We had lunch and then an ice-cream truck came. Regi jokingly waved his hand and the van stopped.

"Sorry, mate," we told Reg, "but now you have to go and buy something from him!"
Poor Reg just had enough coins in his wallet so he bought each one of us ice-cream. Well, Pat is not one for ice-cream but that day, since it was free, he took one. However, he couldn't finish it, so he walked around with it for a while, with big birds following him. Later he threw his ice-cream in the water.

"Why didn't you give it to the birds that followed you?" I asked.

"Oh man, I should have, I'm so stupid!" he replied.

Well that's Patrick! Those who knew him have all seen the weird and amusing things he did. That's who he was. My children and I remember so many funny things that have cracked us laughing all our lives.

After having our ice-cream, we all got into the car and were waiting for dad to come in so we could drive off. He took his time and the birds were still following him.

"What's up—aren't you coming?" I asked.

"The birds have come to say good bye to me—I feel bad for them," he told us.

Finally, he got in and we drove off.

At the cottage we all rested. Pat went into his room and lay down to read the book he had brought. It was Billy Graham's "Been There, Done That, Now What?" I wondered afterwards what he was reading in this book. Was it a coincidence or what?

Then we all watched a cricket match between Australia and Pakistan. We loved our cricket and for fun we always used to tease the Pakistani boys who were like family to us about who would win. While we were enjoying the match, suddenly the power went off. We all went to check what had happened. Then Pat went to the power box and Nigel followed him. They couldn't find any problem and came back. Pat decided to ring the owner of the house and an electrician, but we had to go out to find a phone. Pat also needed a towel so I would get to the shops before they closed. Pat loved his walks and so decided to walk up to find a phone and make the calls. The walk was uphill but he insisted he would do it, while the children decided they would come to the shops with me. On the way, we checked if he was at the petrol station so we could take him as well. He wasn't there so we rushed to the shops and got back in just a few minutes—maybe ten minutes or so.

When we got back everything looked very different. All these cars were in our driveway—the ambulance, the police, and cars belonging to the electrician and the owner of the house. That was why I couldn't believe it really was our driveway when we came back. Patrick had been able to ring the electrician and the house owner and they were there. There wasn't much room for my car but I still pulled in.

Before I could even open my mouth, the ambulance guy asked me, "Are you Mrs Datta?"

"Yes," I said.

"I'm really sorry," he told me, "but I have very bad news for you."

"Yes," I said.

"I'm really sorry," he told me, "but I have a very bad news for you."

What is he talking about, I thought? I don't know anyone here. Maybe someone has sent a message from Sydney. Then he said the worst thing I could ever hear in my life.

"Your husband has just passed away."

The children were with me and my daughter shouted back at him, "Don't ever say that about my dad!"

Then off they ran up the driveway as fast as they could. I ran for my life too up those steps to find him lying there right in front of the door. This was the place where we had dispersed only a few minutes ago and now he was lying there lifeless.

I couldn't believe my eyes.

"Please do something!" I begged those paramedics standing beside him. "Hurry up—please do something fast!"

They had already tried everything to revive him and couldn't do anymore. They told me they had tried many times but it was all over. Just like that, life was over for my darling husband. I sat down there with him, my children beside me. I felt I should do something like pump up air into his lungs so he could breathe. His body was still warm as if he was about to start breathing anytime. Nothing was going to change, according to the paramedics. Even now, almost 13 years have gone by whenever I tell this and how it all happened, my pain comes back as if it had just happened yesterday.

I had no idea how quickly life would change forever for the four of us. I lost the one I loved so much, my dear husband. The children lost their dad. Life is never go ng to be the same. Nobody could ever take his place in our lives.

How could this ever be? How could we live without the most important person in our lives? What about me? How could I live one minute without him? He was all I wanted. How could I ever do things without him? I needed him every moment of my life. My heart was shattered into a million pieces. My mind went round and round in circles, asking thousands of questions. I asked God, "Where were you? Couldn't you save his life? Are you really God? Or am I following you in vain?" I was very angry with God and felt such hatred in my heart for Him. I asked God question after question, but no answer came.

My children had lots to say to dad as he lay there. Nige felt sorry he had asked dad for a drum kit Pat bought for him just before we went up to the mountains. He just said, "I'm so sorry, dad! Did I put too much pressure on you? I'm sorry, dad, wake up please!"

Reg and Haze kept in whatever they felt like saying in their hearts. They just sobbed quietly as they sat with me, wishing dad could get up.

After a while, the paramedics handed a phone to us to call our family. So Haze got up and rang my brother Rajen, who was more like a good friend to Pat than family. Every day they would talk about so many things to do with church or about personal things—but they had to talk. When Haze called, he had the biggest shock and couldn't even talk at first.
"Are you sure?" he asked her. "No, it can't be, are you sure" he had all the same questions as us, but we had no answers. Anyway, who did have the answer?

My brother's family left their home to come over to us, as soon as they heard the news. Thank God they had some visitors for dinner that night. They had a six seater car that could bring them up the mountains. We were two hours away, but my brother told me later it was the longest journey of his life. He had wanted to be there with us that very moment—if only that was possible! All the way, like all of us, he questioned why, what and how all this happened.

My Pakistani sons Wilson, Sohail, Sam and others, (who were like our own adopted children) also drove all the way up to be with us. All our friends who heard about the news turned up, but only my brother and his family were able to see Pat's lifeless body. I begged the paramedics to keep him there right in front of my eyes for as long as they could. At around 10.00pm, however, they had to take him to the Blue Mountains Hospital Morgue. I hated the idea. Strangely I felt I was putting my lovely husband into the place for dead people. However, that was the truth I had to face up to, but I didn't want to. At that moment it was really very difficult to face the fact that truly he was gone, he's dead and not breathing so yes, it was mind blowing to face the reality that that had happened to our beloved husband and daddy.

On the Saturday, there were so many people with us. They decided we all should go back home to Belmore, but I was the first to protest.

"I'm not going to leave my husband behind!" I told them. "I came with him and I'll go with him when he goes."

After much persuasion, however, I had to go, even though I felt so upset that I was leaving him alone. I felt absolutely rotten inside me leaving him behind.

All the way back home, the memories of the event were so fresh. Wasn't it yesterday we went past all those places singing songs, laughing away, talking and having fun? Going back home was so very painful for the children and me. In my heart, I wondered how I could walk into our home without him by my side. What about all the places we had been together? If only I could change this situation for my own sake! "God, please help me here!" I cried. "I need some answers."

When death comes to other people, it's very easy for us to understand from afar. This was too complicated for me! It was such a difficult experience when it came to losing my own husband. Thoughts like now I'm sleeping on my own, where is he, when will he come back and so many thoughts went wild over and over again in my mind every day. This went on for so long and I thought it was going to be there forever. My mind was really going crazy. I had no interest in anything as I felt the most precious thing I had was gone. Many weeks went by without sleep, always I missed him as I felt "he was right here and now he is no more by my side" It felt like life had come to a standstill.

40

God gave me this verse at the Katoomba house when I asked God why couldn't He save Pat? The answer came as a shock to me **'And we know that all things work together for good to those who love God, to those who are called according to His purpose.'** **(Romans 8:28)** I just hated this verse. I didn't know what God was telling me. I was angry with God.

"What does He know about my pain?" I kept asking. "Why is He giving me this verse, if only He knows there is nothing good coming out of this? What good is going to come into my life when I have three teenage children to care for all by myself? Do you know how sick person I am, God? Do you know only Pat can take care of me when I am feeling so bad? You don't seem to know anything anyway."

I was truly angry with God. Hours and hours I fought with God for a few days. I hated Him and didn't want to talk to Him nicely. I didn't open my Bible—I just had question after question. Why? Why? Why?

We arrived at the church manse after a long journey from Katoomba. Our home was the church manse since Patrick was the pastor. We went in and straight away there were crowds of people coming to see us. The news spread far and wide and people poured in so quickly. They all had a message of sympathy but no one could feel my pain. Then a lovely couple walked in hand in hand and I hated them so much. "God, why didn't you choose to separate them? Why it had to be my husband?" I thought. Everyone told me how sorry they were to hear the news of Pat's death. If only their condolences could have brought back my dear hubby.

Hours turned into days and now I was so sick of myself. Often I was talking to myself. Families started to arrive from Canada, New Zealand, Fiji and interstate. They all tried to encourage me. No one could do anything to change my mind or to help my husband come back, not even God as He had more important things to teach me in life.

After all this time of anger and frustration at God and others, I opened my Bible and devotional book. I could not believe my eyes how the devotion I read was just for me. It was amazing, considering these words would have been written many months ago. The fact that God had put these words right in front of my eyes was nothing short of a great miracle. The devotion read: "If you have lost a loved one, you go through lots of pain and suffering in your life. No one will understand your deepest sorrows. This is my promise to you "I will never leave you nor forsake you". People will come and go in our lives, some for a little while or a year or ten years or even fifty years, but I am always there for you. 'I will never leave you nor forsake you even until the end." It also said to me: "Families will be here for only a limited time, but you must trust me and carry on the job (Pat) has left behind."

In Joshua, it was a lesson for me too that Just as, after the death of Moses, Joshua took his place, so I was to carry the baton and go on serving our God. From that day I got up and asked my brother if we could please start a prayer meeting that night so I could hear some words from the Bible. We received so much relief from the Word of God and the prayers we had together.

Patrick, Kushma and the children
Hazel, Regi and Nigel, 1995

Multicultural Ministry, 1999
Belmore Church of Christ
(left to right)
Rajen Prasad, David Kim, Patrick Datta,
Benjamin Kim, Colin Bowser

*My heroine, mum in law,
my faithful role model*

*My beloved husband
"The wind beneath my wings"*

"Like these cloud of witnesses, let us rid ourselves of everything that gets in the way, and of the sin which holds on to us so tightly, and let us run with determination the race that lies before us. Let us keep our eyes fixed on Jesus, on whom our faith depends from beginning to end."

*My earthly father,
"Safe in the Arms of Jesus"*

*My spiritual, dad, mentor and
friend, Dr GD James*

This all knowing God knew me and chose me to go through this biggest test in my life. He knew how I will react and He knew about my frustrations towards Him.  Surely God knew everything in me and He brought me to this stage where I started dealing with the deepest sorrows and pain telling him all my burdens.  Slowly I got better in my thoughts and my life. This is one pain that was heart wrenching, mind blowing and out of my ability.  That's what I thought then. **1Corinthinas 10:13** has a fresh meaning for me now.

**1 Corinthians 10:13  The Everyday Bible (New Century Version)**

**The only temptations that you have are the temptations that all people have. But you can trust God. He will not let you be tempted more than you can stand. But when you are tempted, God will also give you a way to escape that temptation.  Then you will be able to stand it.**

This was the beginning of the healing in my life. This was the day I read the Bible and said to God: "I can't understand anything right now. You will enable me to get through this with your power. I can't do anything but you can." I asked God to forgive my evil thoughts about Him and guide me through all I had to do alone now. As I studied God's Word, I felt so much stronger day by day and was able to strengthen my family and children too. It was a long time of crying, weeping and sleepless nights and by then I had also lost my voice. I thank God for this as I felt like talking to no one except to God. My family took care of everything and I stayed locked in my room, going through Psalm after Psalm, just as David talked to God and prayed for His wisdom. I prayed to God to help my family and for special strength to face the week ahead. God helped me to think clearly and make sense of what was happening. I had to be prepared to face facts now. I told myself: "Nothing will change, so get up and think straight." With God on my side, I knew I had nothing to fear. He holds my children's and my future.

We had prayer meetings where people shared so much about what Pat had done in their spiritual life and it felt so good to hear that so many were challenged, uplifted and encouraged by my dear husband. I could see now that Patrick's time really was over. Now we had to get up and do things for the Lord. Many non-believers were there as well, it was so good to see them hear the word of God. They had been very blessed too—it was amazing to hear about the things Pat was doing in their lives. It didn't matter to Pat whether they were Indian, Korean, Chinese, Filipino, Burmese, Pakistani, Anglo-Saxon or any other nationality. He loved them all and worked for all of them. Many people shared and we heard so many lovely stories from my husband's life. Slowly the burdens start to feel lighter on my shoulders. It was as if I had been carrying a big piece of log on my shoulder all alone and now others had come along and lifted it together with me. It was getting better.

We heard some funny stories about my husband too and we all laughed our heads off. We also had lots of family staying in our home and they all had some weird experience with Pat that they told that night. There was so much laughter we were scared the neighbours would tell us off. I started to feel so much better now that we were all sharing the burden. I was so thankful for all my family and the many things they did to ease the pain in my heart.

People were so kind they bought and prepared food for days. They cared for our visitors and us as a family. That really meant so much to us. I don't know where they all came from but the church was full every night for prayer meetings. I really appreciated their thoughtfulness to us—we needed their support.

We had Pat's funeral at the Pinegrove Cemetery. Two years earlier, his mother had also been buried there. The service beforehand was at the Belmore Church of Christ and we had a massive crowd of more than seven hundred in attendance at this funeral service. The church was then ninety-six years old but never in its history had the church (I was told later) seen a crowd like that in this building. People of all different nationalities came from far and wide to farewell Patrick.

All my children went up and spoke so proudly of their dad in front of all these people. I didn't have the courage to do this but after hearing my children, I went up as well to speak about all that my dear husband had done in our lives. It was heartbreaking to see him in the coffin. Even at that point, I wished he could get up and start talking but sadly we had to say goodbye to him forever. This pain will stay in my heart and even as I write this, all the painful memories have come back. As the years have gone by since then, I have chosen to think of all the lovely times we had together and that is what has carried me through. I know I will definitely meet him in Heaven again one day. What a blessed hope we have in Christ and the His Word!

A few weeks after the funeral, I went back into doubting mode again. What if I didn't see my husband again? What if the Bible is wrong? What if there is no Heaven? Then I took courage and searched for my own benefit, all the Bible verses about Heaven. I was truly amazed how many things I found about Heaven- the fact that there will be no pain, sorrow and death there. Then I began thinking of how Patrick had preached all his life about this Heaven where he had now gone. Billy Graham, Luis Palau, the Wesley brothers way back in history—they all preached the same message. Why would they do it if it was false? My mother-in-law's living faith was outstanding—why would she pray if we have a dead God? There was no way they could all be wrong. What about my dear dad, Dr GD James? He spent all his life preaching about this same God. Why would he waste his time?

One outstanding thing that happened was that one of our friends we had been witnessing to for years was at the funeral and heard us all speaking. He was a strong Hindu priest and very strong in his beliefs. As I saw the crowd there, I wanted to share the Gospel in case there would be people present who didn't know Christ. I mentioned how Patrick preached Christ and His death and resurrection and how Jesus is making a home in Heaven for us. I shared that Patrick had gone ahead of me but that I will see him in Heaven because I trust in Jesus.

If you too want to see him there, you need to seek Christ who is in Heaven and who wants all of us to go there, I mentioned what Jesus said in **John 14:6, 'I am the way, the truth and the life; no one comes to the Father except through me.'**

After the church service, this seventy-five year old Hindu priest said something very interesting "I've officiated many funerals in all my life, but today what I have seen is beyond comprehension. How is it possible that there is such a huge crowd to farewell Patrick? Many different nationalities have all worked together in love and harmony right throughout this funeral. Something is very different in here—it blows my mind. I have never been to such a funeral—I'm so glad I'm here to see this for myself."

This was great to hear. My prayer was for his salvation and others as well, that they see Jesus through us. I wanted this funeral to be a testimony to all who were present.
We had many more people—about three hundred or so—waiting for us at the grave side. The service there was wonderful too. In all we shared there, we wanted Christ be given glory for the life of His servant Patrick.

It's never easy to say goodbye to anyone like this, let alone to my husband. I never understood the pain and sorrow that keeps on nagging, day after day. One minute I was fine and the next something would trigger a lovely memory and I would start crying again. This went on and on for a very long time. Every birthday celebration, we wished dad was there for his children— their twenty-first parties, their graduations, their engagements, their weddings, and also the birth of his grandchild. He has missed all this and we have missed him. We wish he were here to see and jump up and down in excitement as he usually did.  Maybe he has a better view from up there!

God has taught me so much every step of the way. Even though it was hard, I learnt to trust in Him even in this sudden death of my husband. All the pain and suffering as I look back now was only to train me for the future in the Lord's work. At that time it felt too much to bear but nothing is too much, compared to what suffering Christ had to go through. I want to personalize the following verse for myself:

**1 Peter 1:6–7** says to me:

**So be truly glad, there is wonderful joy ahead, even though you (*Kushma*) have to endure many trials for a little while. These trials will show that your (*Kushma*) faith is genuine. It is being tested as fire tests and purifies gold—your (*Kushma*) faith is far more precious than mere gold.  When your (*Kushma*) faith remains strong through many trials, it will bring you (*Kushma*) much praise and glory and honour on the day when Jesus Christ is revealed to the whole world.**

**The Funny Side of Patrick**

When Pat and I became serious about getting married, together with my brother and sister-in-law we went to visit my sister in Sigatoka. The six of us all went in the one car and we drove around visiting some tourist places like hotels. In one of the hotels there was a beautiful, big swimming pool. Pat was trying to impress my family as much as he could, to show what a brilliant guy I had caught. It was his first visit to meet my family. The pool water was very still.

"You know there's no water in this pool—it's empty," he said to us all. "I'll show you." When he stepped onto the third step, he discovered there certainly was water in it! You should have seen his face—not to mention his wet pants and new pair of shoes that he had to wear all the way back home! Talk about embarrassed! As usual, he started wiping his glasses and didn't know whether to talk or be quiet as he felt so rotten inside. There went all the good impression.

I'm so grateful for the many things Patrick did in his life that made us laugh and laugh. Even today we remember all the fun he created with his words and actions. This was one aspect of his life that is truly very memorable. How can we forget? You may think it so stupid but he was a character—a character like Ray Romano in 'Everybody loves Raymond'. He made so many silly mistakes but when we asked why, he would pretend and say, "I just wanted to make you all laugh and enjoy it!"

My brother's house was only a five minute walk away. I needed to have a little break by myself and rest for two hours because I was really exhausted, so I decided to go to his place.

"The house is yours," I told Patrick. "And the children need you just for this afternoon. "But don't ring me—and don't try to drop by with any excuses."

"I'll try," he said.

Even before I arrived there, Patrick had already called twice.

"Is she there yet?"

"Who?" my brother asked.

 "Kush is coming to rest at your place."

"Well, she's not here yet."

As I arrived at the door my brother handed over the phone to me, telling me it's Pat.

"Why have you rung?" I asked him.

"I don't know where the salt is. And where's the rice?"

"Well, I haven't brought it with me, so it must be in the kitchen cupboard  Tell me, why did you "really" ring?"

"I miss your voice around here," he told me.

It was only five minutes since I left and this is what he does! Oh, I love him so much that he could think of missing me even after such a short time!  What about me, it's thirteen years now. How can I live without him?  "Doing it God's way"

Back home during this same incident, Haze was keeping an eye on her dad hoping he would not call me. When she sneaked into the living room, she saw her dad with the remote control in his hand, trying to dial a number again and again! She laughed and laughed and threw herself into the living room.

"Dad, is that a phone?" she burst out.

"Oh, silly me!!" said Dad, looking at it.

"See, Dad?" Haze told him. "You weren't supposed to ring mum and now even God is telling you not to dial out!"

I feel so embarrassed sharing the silly things Pat did—but do other people make mistakes like this? Perhaps not! On the other hand, maybe some of you are feeling relieved that someone else did the same silly things you do and there was another man in the world like you!

I mentioned earlier how we prepared to go to New Zealand to work but did not go in the end. We knew we were running away from God. As usual, we had to have medicals done for all the family members. We had all the blood and urine tests done and then they asked for a stool (poo) specimen. In those days in Fiji, they didn't provide the containers for this. They advised us to put it in a little ice cream tub with the lid on. So we bought each person ice cream to eat and then to use the containers. We had to clean it and take the specimen in the morning. I told the children what to do and they all did a great job. I had to take this to the doctor in the morning. They all left for school and I collected the containers and left. The doctor opened them and everything was fine, except the last one which belonged to Pat was full to the brim. The doctor looked at me and shook his head!  As for me, I wanted to drop dead in front of him. I laughed all the way to Patrick's office and told him what the doctor's reaction was.

"Didn't he tell us to empty the container and fill it up?" he said.

I understand we are only human. We laugh at all the funny shows but don't we all do the most stupid things in life?

Patrick disliked shopping all his life. Once I asked all my family to come shopping with me for underwear  that was on sale.  I asked everyone to choose their own and meet up at the checkout.  It was all good as children never had done this before neither had Patrick. I was the one getting their stuff all the time, with a tight budget there was no choice. When we got home from our shopping trip, we all showed what we had bought. Patrick came out to demonstrate what he had bought for himself. He paraded with this red G-string wearing it back to front, on top of his pants.  He said "can you guys tell me what is the point of these undies?" You should have seen Hazel, Nige and Regi, we all laughed till we collapsed.

This actually happened a week before Pat died.  After the funeral you should have seen the boys acting out what Pat had been up to lately.

We had lots of stray dogs around our place in Fiji. There were times these dogs would have their puppy under our house.  We ended up with lots of puppies many times.  It was a lot of work.  One time there were two little pups which were very weak and one of them died. The other was almost dead, his breathing was very low. I ask Pat to please bury the dead puppy. He went and buried both of them, even the one who was still breathing! After he told me "I buried both of them" I asked "was the other pup dead? He said "no, but he would die eventually" I went and dug him out and poor pup was still breathing very softly. Just as well Pat didn't put too much mud over him! I reminded him "how would you feel if someone buried you alive?" and he laughed.

After the funeral, all these stories came up. The whole lot of us went wild with laughter. This was really good for us after all the crying we did. Everyone in the room had a funny experience with Pat and that night we all had fun at his expense. Our children didn't know all the funny things dad had done in his younger life so it was good for us al  to have a night of just pure laughter. This truly was the medicine we needed after such a heavy, painful week. Praise God even for this experience!

I have told you something of Pat's funny side in this book. Just to be fair I must tell you something of my funny side as well. Whenever I use any public toilets, I make sure to wrap the toilet seat with lots of toilet paper before I sit on it. One time, my very precious sister-in-law Ruth and I went out to Manly for the day. Ruth is my husband's youngest sister. Both of us have been great friends all our lives. She understands all I go through and when she goes through problems in life she calls me from Brisbane and talks for hours. When Ruth's husband passed away, she spent a lot of time with me in Sydney. We loved going out to new places and this time we went to Manly.

After lunch, I went to the rest room and did as I always used do—cover the seat with toilet paper. I used the toilet and went out and went into some shops on the way to the Manly wharf, walking side by side with my sister in law. Suddenly, she moved back a little behind me and saw this long strip of toilet paper hanging from my pants to the ground like a tail. She was laughing her head off as she stared at my back and I looked to see what she was laughing at. What a shock!  It was not funny to me but totally embarrassing! What a disaster that was for me! Both of us laughed all the way home. Ruth had to tell this to my children, so together we all laughed again. In no time this story went worldwide to all my families abroad.

Thank God we didn't have face book then as it would have been worse. I'm sure Patrick would have been really happy for once that I acted so stupidly like a big fool. I feel we all have to laugh and be able to enjoy life and live this life to the fullest. Patrick did this for sure and now I'm learning to laugh and enjoy every moment God has given us. We don't know when we will be called home so let's enjoy life while we can.

*At the wedding of Pradeep Narayan
one of our disciples, 2010
(from left)
Mum, Kushma, Rajen (brother), Pradeep*

# Tributes to Patrick

When Patrick left us, many of our families, friends, church members and acquaintances supported us through prayer and kindness. The students we ministered to long time ago, now much older, married and are serving the Lord. They have encouraged me and my family a great deal in my darkest days. What we taught them in life a long time ago has come back to us in such gracious ways I can never imagine. Thank you all.

He was a sincere believer in Christ, and was always searching the scriptures for depth and insight into new truths for himself and to teach others. Thus he spent many hours preparing his sermons and Bible lessons which he faithfully delivered with passion so that the hearers learnt and became true dedicated followers of the Lord Jesus.

Patrick made a remarkable impression in my life from my first meeting with him in 1973, when I went from Labasa to Deuba to a Brethren  Bible School. He shared genuine warmth and friendship to a country boy; this touched my heart, as I could feel real Christian love and acceptance. His teachings were simple yet conveyed such depth and meaning. His companion, (the guitar) made his songs famous and continued to touch the hearts of many both young and old for Jesus.

Our friendship grew and I invited him to be my best man at my wedding in 1974. While he was there he held the bridesmaid's hand and some magic happened. Two years later Patrick became my bother-in-law by marrying my dear sister Kushma. They have served the Lord together for many years in Fiji and in Australia.

As Jesus said about Nathanial "There is no guile in him" so was Patrick.
A true follower became leader, lead many to Christ and discipled them.
With true compassion of heart, Patrick and Kushma went into many squatter settlements in Fiji to reach out to the poor, needy and the sick, sharing the love of Jesus Christ in many practical ways. Many of these people who were touched by them, I have met in recent years are now living successful lives for the Lord both here in Fiji and overseas.
What a tribute to a caring and godly man, an amazing legacy left for his children, grandchildren and others to follow.
To God be the glory!

**Shiu Narain**
Compassion for Fiji Children
Rakiraki Fiji
shiunarayan@hotmail.com

I thank God for people like you and brother Patrick for the love and compassion you showed to me as well as my family. I was in high school in the mid 80's. You reflected what true Christianity is. As a Hindu I admired people like you and your late husband. You both had a genuine interest in helping me when I could not afford the school fees. My father was paralysed for 6 years. I grew up without my father's care and love since the age of 14. It was a very difficult time. I did not have my father's love or an elder brother to look up to. That is when I went into wrong company, became rebellious to authority and was very angry (hurt) looking at my father's condition. This was the reason I got into so much mischief in school. In spite of my rebellious nature, I always respected both you and Patrick for your love, patience and kindness towards me. Both you and Patrick sowed the seed in my heart during the scripture classes. That seed did not die but sprang up to be a big tree in God's own timing. Thank you for believing in me and making a difference in my life.

Today God has blessed me with a beautiful family and a good ministry. God used me to pioneer two churches here in Sydney and to build one orphanage in India with 25 orphans fully sponsored by members of our church. To God be the Glory!

**Shalen Sharma**
Senior Pastor
Lighthouse community Care
Sydney Australia


*I do have a soft spot for you and will do whatever I can to help. Kushma and I do love you and will be there for you always*
The letter was signed off as "Pat, the Bengali."

This self nominated "Bengali' was my brother-in-law. I fondly called him Jeejaa. He wrote me this letter whilst I was going through an intricate phase in my life in 1997. This letter reminds me how Jeejaa demonstrated his trust in the LORD in the face of adversity, which was with grace, peace and faith in the Almighty. Jeejaa's absence is deeply felt whenever I visit my sister and on every family gatherings.

I thank the LORD for Jeejaa Pat, for giving me the privilege of knowing him. Beyond the joys of knowing him, I was profoundly impacted by his life, in so much more ways than anyone could imagine.

Jeejaa, You haven't really died, only fallen asleep….and you have done so with grace, and with a heart filled with love for everyone who knew you, I can confidently say that for you, to live was CHRIST, and to die was gain.

Au Revoir, My Bengali Jeejaa - will catcha later in heaven - Roshni

**Roshni Kumar (my youngest sister)**
Watch House Officer
New Zealand.

***Many people cross our path in our journey of life. Few leave a lasting impression on us. Patrick Datta was one such man.***

I had never done well in my studies and topping the class was always a dream never fulfilled. During one of the scripture classes, Patrick was teaching from the Epistle of James and emphasized the scripture "If any of you  lack wisdom, you should ask God, who gives generously to all without finding fault, and it will be given to you" (James 1:5) I believed that scripture and I silently prayed and asked God for wisdom and knowledge. That scripture, that silent prayer changed my life. I topped the class from Form 3 to Form 6, become the Head boy of Gospel High School, ended the year as the Dux of the school. Patrick also taught us that "God would always honour those who honour Him." This was another of the lessons that I took to heart.  I have seen the power of that statement in my life – God has brought me honour and His blessings plus favour in my life as I serve him.

Patrick was a giver – His actions matched what he taught.  In 1979, our school had planned a day trip to visit the new Hydro Dam that was being built at Monasavu.  It is situated in the interior of Viti Levu which is the main island in Fiji. I really wanted to go but could not afford the bus fare. I came from a poor family where everyday, survival was a challenge. Patrick asked me if I was going, and when I said "no," he immediately took out a five dollar note. With thankful heart I took the money, paid my fare to go.  It was one of the best days of my life – I was able to see such a magnificent development in my country thanks to the generosity that Patrick showed me. It was later I learnt that not only was I a recipient of his generosity but Patrick  together with his family, were always seeking out and providing for people in need.

His greatest investment was in the Kingdom of God and in people like me. Many boys gave their lives to God at the boys' camps every year. These camps were highlights for us every year.  I was challenged to serve God early in my life through his teaching, mentoring and spending his precious time with us boys at his home in Flagstaff.  No words can describe of his passion, self-less love and care for us all.  Patrick's life has impacted many in our schools, churches and everywhere he went. He made a difference in countless lives. To God be the Glory!

**Johnson Mustafa Gani**
Assistant Pastor
Agape Revival Centre
Fiji

Patrick was a man of prayer. We prayed for all matters in life. I was just 30. He helped me to become a mature spiritual servant of the Lord. Whenever I face hard times in the ministry even now, those prayers we both prayed, has reinforced my faith in the Lord and His work here.

The best thing was he loved teasing and having fun with friends.  I think no one wants a boring life though we are serving the King of kings. Life should be fun even in hard times. Patrick would create that kind of atmosphere among the friends. Now I always look for something fun in my current ministry.

He managed well his family as he was grounded in love and prayers. Now I am like him a servant with a big family. The way he loved his wife, Kushma and his love for the children was remarkable and admirable.  I am sure if he were watching from heaven, he would be very happy with his family. His servant-hood, fun and excitement will always be remembered by all of us who knew him and in the hearts of many in the hostel in this golden land.

**Lian Zam**
Dagon Community Centre
Myanmar


Patrick Datta played a significant role in nurturing me in my journey as a young Christian.

I remember the many visits we would make to his house and the many hours we spent together having fellowship over dinner. The trip to Labasa was a memorable trip and over a week as I travelled with him, stayed with him, witnessed first-hand the Christian love and hospitality of Patrick and his extended family. I also recall the many hours we spent together in playing Hindi Christian songs on the guitar. Patrick was a great musician and my early inspiration for learning the guitar came from him. He also sang at my wedding and prayed for God's blessing on Madhu and me.

On hearing the news of his shocking death, I really felt I lost a great friend and a mentor, who to me was a living example of Christianity in action. His teachings and practical demonstration of Christian love have left a permanent legacy in my life. I count it a great privilege to thank God for allowing Patrick to do the good work he did in my life. Patrick's legacy will live on in my life and that of my family. The seeds he sowed in my life will continue to bear fruit as long as I journey through this life.

**Vijendra Lal**
 Principal Education Officer
TAFE NSW
Sydney Australia

## Camaraderie all the way to Sydney

Patrick and Kushma Datta, a newly married couple, opened their hearts, their lives and their home for me.  Their love for Jesus Christ was laid bare, as they encouraged and guided a young convert into a practicing Christian.

Lots of Bible studies, hospitality, caring and loving attitude towards young Christians held us together. Their commitment and sincerity kept the youth of the Assemblies in unison. They were our leaders and our mentors. They groomed us, through their faithful training, as key Sunday school teachers and youth leaders. Patrick was an inspiration!

They served the Lord with dignity, nurturing us for His service and guided us to be strong for Jesus. Having a young family did not deter from their sacred calling. They recognized the pre-eminence of their Lord. The strength and discipleship of my early days stayed with me in my new life in a new country in Australia.

Together with my husband, we were able to assist the Datta family to settle in this country when they arrived for further studies at Emmaus Bible College, Epping. NSW, Australia. They were a great force and channel of blessings to Concord Community Church. We valued their devotion and support. We learnt a lot from this dedicated Christian couple. To God be the Glory!

**Vijay Poonan**
Concord Community Church
Sydney Australia

Many more tributes have been sent to me by my families, fr ends, our ex-students, our disciples, church members and my multi- ethnic children from all over the world. Your words of encouragement, kind thoughts and prayers mean a lot to my family and me.  I do apologize for not using all of your tributes.

*Nigel's "graduation" from kindergarten
with Hazel and Reginel, 1990*

*Nigel's graduation, Macquarie University, 2006
Hazel, Nigel, Kushma, Reginel*

# 9 The Year of the "Plagues"

In this same year (2000), after the funeral was over and we picked up our lives slowly, more things happened like the plagues of Egypt. The year started with many problems. In March when we received the postmortem results of Patrick, we were asked to see our heart specialist in case our children had inherited the same heart problem as Pat. We all went, and when they tested my three children, we found out that Nigel had a heart problem. This came as a shock and hit me really hard. How could this be?

"God, what are you doing? Wasn't it enough that Pat had this problem and now I have my son with heart problem as well! He'll have this problem all his life," I protested to Him.

God granted us the wisdom to do things differently. Later we found out that his heart is not as bad as his father's was. He doesn't even need to have any surgery. Praise God for this! A month later Regi, my youngest child, broke his ankle very badly. His leg was swollen like a balloon. We rushed him to hospital. He had emergency surgery to fix him. The doctors used some plates and metals to fix it. His leg was in cast for six weeks. I did everything for him as he couldn't do much, taking him every few days for check-ups, then to school so he didn't miss out too much in school work. He was much better when his cast was out. We thank God he managed on his own.

My health wasn't too good with all the stress I had gone throughout that time. I had some bleeding problems even before Patrick died. Now this problem had become worse. The doctors suggested a hysterectomy. My three children took care of me while I was in hospital. Hazel was a very responsible daughter. She drove the boys to see me, took them to school and she even cooked for me. They spent many hours lying with me in the hospital bed. Thank God for friends and families who were able to visit and encourage me! The doctors tried some medication before the surgery and it worked, so thankfully in the end, they didn't have to do the hysterectomy.

Later in the year on the eve of Father's day, our house was raided by burglars. All the things they took were things my husband had recently bought for our family—a new TV, a stereo, a DVD and video player and lots of things from Hazel's room. Everything that was sentimental to us was gone. All our lives, we could not afford new things. We always made do with 'hand me down' stuff. When we came to Belmore Church, this was the first paid work we had since 1976 when we went into full-time ministry. For the first time we had something new and now it was all gone. We were all too terrified to even go inside the house. The police took a statement and off they went. The glass door was shattered and it was all over the place. My dear brother Rajen always took good care of my family, anytime, anywhere, he was there! This time he nailed some temporary timber on the front door. All night we huddled together as the kids slept, I kept a watch over the place. I was terrified the whole night.

I really thank my brother for always being there for me all my life. Many times he had to care for two families, his own plus mine. He made sure all was going well with my family especially after Pat's passing. May God bless you chotanna (brother).

The day after the burglary was Sunday. Haze told me, she was not going to church anymore.

"This God didn't even protect our place. It's just too much now, mum! First it was dad and now this. I don't even know whether there is any God."

I pointed out to her that we were all safe—at least we had not been there to face the thieves. What if they had raped us and beaten us or shot us? Thank God we were out. These things are worldly things, material things we can get again, but if we had been emotionally tarnished, our lives would have been ruined forever. She then agreed how true this is and was feeling much better.

We all went to the morning worship service. Soon people came to know what had happened. By the end of Sunday we had two huge TVs and three DVD players and many other things people gave us. How wonderful was this? We need to be grateful in all circumstances. My children saw God's goodness on us through these things and realized it is good to be in God's family.

One great thing that happened in September that year was the Olympic Games. In memory of Pat, who was keen in Olympic Games, we as a family decided we would go and watch some of the games. Just to be there was an amazing feeling. The mood of the Olympics, the beautiful colours, the flags, the people from all over the world cheering for their teams was overwhelming. We loved being there and wished Pat was with us, but maybe "he had a better view from up in Heaven." On every occasion we missed dad, we would say the same that he is definitely watching us from up there in Heaven!

*Hazel's Wedding, 2005*
*Anita, Tanya, Hazel, Cheryl*

# 10   Hazel's Wedding

When Hazel did her practical teaching in some schools, she came back home, saying "Mum, I'll never go back to that school. The children are so bad, they swear and throw things and have no respect." I had to remind her of the broken backgrounds the children came from.

"How blessed are we that our parents taught us well," she commented.
God is great and has been teaching us together as a family to support one another in difficult circumstances.

When Haze went to do her practical teaching in a Christian school, she loved the environment, the teachers and the work there.

"I wish I could get a position in this school," she told me.

"We will pray and God will provide," I answered.

She kept telling me that no one in this school wanted to leave as the school was really good. I reminded her that we have a great God—someone might get pregnant or someone will definitely leave for some reason. I continued to pray for her future in teaching. Then one day, the Principal rang from the school and told Hazel that if by chance she wasn't getting married during the school term, then the job was hers. Haze already had set up a date for her wedding and it happened to be during the school term. I suggested we change the wedding date and take up this job, despite the fact that we had paid a deposit at the reception place.

"It doesn't matter," I told them both. "We can change the venue but we can't let this job go. This is the answer from God that we have been praying for so long. He has given you the job, now it's up to you to take it." This was a true test for Hazel as to what she will choose. She did accept the offer and many blessings followed. Praise God He heard our prayers!
I had been praying for a godly person to marry Haze. When Haze saw all of her friends with boyfriends, she would keep telling me she wasn't beautiful, that's why no one loved her. I reminded her that in God's timing He would bring the perfect person to her. Praise God He did answer my prayers even if we didn't know where this person would come from. God had prepared him well before we knew it. This has been my prayer for all my children. I don't know where God will bring the person from, but I know He will at the right time.

God in His own time brought this person into Hazel's life. He worked in Target with Hazel's university friend. She kept asking Hazel to meet this person but Haze kept saying no all the time. One day when Haze rang to talk to this friend, Aaron was chatting online with her.  She got Hazel to chat to Aaron as well. They chatted online—and yes!  Praise God they were in love in no time. Well, well, you should see the book they made of all their online chatting! Later Haze got some photos of him. I was very impressed to see him. One thing I didn't know then was how spiritual he was. I kept praying, even when he came to our home, we prayed for things in their lives, also for their future together, if this was of God.  Hazel had a great impact on his Christian life, as he told Haze.  I'm very blessed to have such a great, godly person in our family now. I'm also very grateful to God that Aaron has a lovely family—mum, dad and a sister Anita. We are really blessed to have such great, spiritual people in our lives. Waiting on God has been a great blessing.

Haze took the job at this wonderful Christian school. We cancelled the wedding reception at the function centre. She was worried about whether we would find another good place. I prayed: "God, You know everything and you will provide." God gave us more than we even thought or could imagine. The centre we found was much cheaper, the food was much better, the dance floor was great and even the seating arrangement worked much better than the other place. We were really blessed by God in all this. How great is our God and how marvellous are His works! He knows more than we do ourselves. You may not ever know how I prayed for every little detail of the wedding.  God surely took care of all those details. It was a wedding to remember!

The wedding was such a wonderful time for me to celebrate my daughter's life. Now was the time to say goodbye to the one I gave birth to and raised up as a wonderful young lady. Now someone else was taking her away from me. Initially it was very difficult for me to think a stranger taking her away. When the two of them would go to Aaron's place or go out for dinner, my heart would cry out as I didn't want her to leave me. Already I felt our family was getting smaller without dad. Now it was tough on me to let go of her. I would cry my heart out when they were gone away. Then consoled myself, saying God has blessed her all this time. He will in her future too. As I came to know what a great and wonderful gentleman Aaron is, my fears all went away. I was able to let go of her without any doubt that they would be happy together.

This is only because both of them love the Lord and serve Him faithfully. Praise God for such a wonderful blessing in giving me a most wonderful son in Aaron. He keeps an eye on me, asking how my health is or if I have any problems. He is always ready to listen to anything I have in my heart. What a lovely blessing from God! Only God knew who to choose to come into my family. I'm so blessed to have him teach me to use the Internet.  If ever I have problems he always fixes the problems for me. I'm writing this book now and if I didn't have any knowledge of the computer I would never be able to do this. It is only through Aaron's constant support, his encouragement and help I have been able to do this book.

Haze and Aaron had been married for five years and were trying to have a baby. Soon the months had turned into years. As we continued to pray, at one stage we thought God had forgotten us. It was hard for us to see Hazel's friends having children, but it became too difficult for her to bear this pain of not having a child of their own. So many godly people prayed too for her but nothing happened. I had collected some baby clothes and would hold these up and pray, begging God for a baby. Haze and Aaron felt like giving up everything as nothing was happening. Eventually, the doctors told them they couldn't have children and this shattered their dream. Both Aaron's parents and I were very shocked to hear this news. But I kept reminding God and praying that one day it would happen. I wrote a letter to God and left it with the baby clothes, asking God: "When is the right time?"

However much we prayed, it was only God who could see the beginning from the end of our lives. He knew when the time would be perfect for the baby to come. God knows the beginning from the end and he knows the puzzles He puts in our lives and fits them all together. When will be the best time for Haze and Aaron and for all of us to have this baby in the family?

# 11   A Bountiful Year

The year 2010 was another big year for my family. After celebrating the tenth memorial service of Patrick with our beloved families in Myanmar (Burma), I arrived home in Australia in January. The celebration was attended by more than four hundred Burmese friends. They all knew Patrick well through Lian who was a Christian brother to Patrick from the Emmaus School days.

While still in Burma, I knew Haze was to hear from the doctor on 4th January. I kept checking the emails to find out if she could conceive or not. This was to be an IVF baby and with this first try, there was an eighty to ninety percent chance of conceiving. When I heard it didn't work out, I was shattered. Haze went through many injections, painful procedures plus everything was really expensive. She hated needles, persevered through it all for the sake of having a baby. But now what? I didn't know what to say to God. I felt hurt as I was so sure that now was the time this baby was going to come. Even now was not the right time. My Burmese friends saw me very disturbed. I could not be my normal self as I suffered inside. I shared what I was going through. We all prayed together that God would help us understand what His will is in our lives.

Haze and Aaron decided they would give it another try with IVF, but the doctor told them that the chances of having a baby this time were very low—maybe only thirty percent.  We all continued to pray. Many people joined us in prayer for the baby to be conceived. When the doctor thought the chances were slim, God intervened and Haze conceived.

What a great miracle this was! What is impossible with man is possible with our great God! God definitely wanted us to trust Him rather than the doctor. Truly the desires of our hearts were fulfilled by this wonderful God. Amazing things happened while Haze grew bigger by day. The amount of things that started coming in for the baby seemed endless. Everything he needed was provided by friends and family members—God used them all to provide all these beautiful things. We were very excited. Aaron's mum and dad and I as grandparents waited impatiently for the arrival of the baby. Hazel had a very good pregnancy with hardly any problems.

Two weeks before the baby's arrival, Haze was suddenly admitted to hospital. She had some kind of liver problem. It was very serious problem. This could cost the baby's life and her own in particular. They kept her overnight for observation. Things didn't change so the doctor's decided they would do an emergency caesarean to get the baby out for Hazel's sake. She was already thirty-eight weeks anyway so we were happy that the baby was full term.

Zachariah Aaron Niranjan was born on 29th October 2010 at 11.31am. It was great to have the baby born on this day. My heart was in pain as my daughter's life was still in great danger. What would come of it all? After a few hours of recovery, when I realized my Haze was out of danger, I was able to celebrate the arrival of my little grandson.

As my only daughter, she has been my very precious gem. I know it might sound selfish, but if I had a choice between saving the mother's or the baby's life, I would choose my daughter. I'm sure they could have more children later but she was too precious for me to let go. God amazingly gave us both. I praise my God for His wisdom and knowledge of our heart's desire. He provided us with this special little prince. Fortunately, the doctors realized that after Hazel's placenta was removed, the liver function readings became normal again. The reading had been extremely high before delivery and there was the danger of kidney failure for Hazel. All the miracles were done by our Heavenly Father as we praise God for His intervention. All is well; Zachariah is a strong and healthy baby. God has blessed him with a lovely mum and dad. He is a very contented baby. He seems to be like Aaron in character— so calm and patient and happy. He is able to go with his parents and enjoy the company of other people, smiling at everyone. We the grandparents adore this precious gift from God.

This is a mystery of having a baby born in a family. What a joy he brings to all the families. When we see how wonderfully the baby was made, how he was knitted together in his mother's womb, it is a great mystery! Even before he was one day old God knew him very well. He even knows the number of years of this baby's life and for that matter ours too. I want to give Him back all He has given me in my life. All my time as well as my energy is to be used to live for Him all the days of my life. Praise God!

I see God's mighty hands on all these things as well as the timing was perfect. Only God knew when the baby should be born. Hazel was still on maternity leave and Zac was growing bigger, very well settled with the baby with his routine. This is when my foot surgery happened.  I was in a lot of pain with some complications as well. Hazel took great care of my needs. The good thing was I really got close to baby Zac. We talked our own language and made him laugh. This recovery time was the best as I had the baby to distract me from pain. I had more time with the baby while others did their own things. Hazel had a "big baby" now. She cared for me and the baby. The way she handled everything I was amazed. In every little detail she was spotless, clean and just the way I like it. She did everything with a smile and with joy.

I have no idea how she had the strength to take care of us all but she did it with all her heart. I'll never forget this experience. She even got Reg, her brother to come over to stay with us when he got sick. Here was a young mother caring for all the sick ones. Think of a house full of people, one with foot surgery, one with a severe ear problem and then a new baby. I don't know how she did it but she did it very well. She is definitely very organized with the baby. It's great to see what a wonderful mother she has become. God truly is an amazing God!

Today I feel so loved, as Zac runs to me when he sees me from afar. Someone who loves me like that makes my life worth living. During play time when I would sometimes pretend to sleep, he would try to lift my head with his little hands and kiss me to wake me, as if to say, "Get up, Nani—I need you here!" He's always ready for a chasing game.  He keeps hugging and kissing me all day long—how wonderful is this love! Such pure love!

When he enters my home he runs in first climbs up on the wheelchair and wants me to read a book. He goes to his toy container pulling out everything to play. He goes through my kitchen pantry. He gets all the groceries out putting it on the floor.  Fortunately my daughter is training him to put things away after using them. He puts them back. He loves to sweep the floor with a broom, wants to vacuum clean the house and cook. Hazel lets him do everything he likes to do. I hope he will do all these jobs later in life like his dad. I thank God for this great gift that has come into our lives. Zac entertains us all day long. He truly is a miracle baby. No one else but God could do such a miracle. We depend on all the medical things but yet God really had His way for this baby. There is a verse in Proverbs that says: "Man makes plan but God has the final say." We can do great things and plan forever for things to happen in our lives but it is only when God opens the door then everything falls into right place. We prayed for months and years but God knew the right time, the perfect time. Praise God—He knows what's best for our lives.

Without my husband by my side, God was the best option for me every moment of the day. In every decision I made, I'm glad I had the best person helping me.

Six weeks after the baby was born, we were at Nigel's wedding. By now Haze was well enough to travel to Brisbane for the wedding. The baby was happy going everywhere we went.

Nigel's Wedding 2010 .

Long before Nigel even mentioned about marriage, I have been praying for him. As I said before I prayed for my children's future partners well before it all happened. Things like this are such an important part of our lives.  Marriage is a life-long commitment.  We need someone who is compatible and will be good for each other.  Where could we run to, to find this person for Nigel?  Only to this God! Hasn't He made the Universe and put the stars in the sky, He knows them all by name. Only this God knows every human being He created. He can find the right person for Nigel.

One Sunday when Nigel was in Canada, we had a visitor in our Church.  She was from Brisbane.  She was talking to everyone and looked very gracious to me. We had known her parents from back in Fiji. This girl I had not seen for 20 years. I knew the baby version of her. She had grown up looking great.  I just said a secret prayer for Nigel as he wasn't here. "Lord this girl is so much like us, do you think she can be the one for Nigel?" I prayed this prayer and left it. After Church she came for lunch to our place. You should have seen all my youth members flocked around her. God knows the best I thought. When Nigel called from Canada I mentioned to him about this girl who may be good for him, he got excited. We left everything there.

One year later, some visitors came from Brisbane to visit us. This happened to be the parents of Shazza. We knew them from many years. When they met Nigel that night everything changed for both Nigel and Shazza. All the cousins got together to catch up for that night. These two spent hours in talking through the night. Nigel came back, he told me, "Mum I have found the person I would like to marry" I was really happy as that was my prayer for him. Thank God!

Nigel had been a wonderful help to me when Haze was married and even before that. It was like his dad was being with me all the way through the tough times. He was very responsible in the times when I had to make difficult decisions. He was one who would tell me when I was doing something wrong. He was now my helpmeet.  I appreciated his understanding my heart. He would always hug me and show his love and kindness to me. He was always there for me, just like Patrick in many ways. For me to let go of Nigel was such a huge thing. I would sit outside in our balcony and cry out to God: "How will I let my son go?" Even when he started talking about moving out, it was very difficult for me. I kept on reading the Bible, praying and reminding myself this is what God wants.  It is God's command for children to be married and live separately.  God filled me with His wisdom from on high to let go of him gracefully. Praise God for that. I was really grateful that Nigel kept me involved in the planning of his wedding. He showed me his new home as well. This meant a lot to me.

Nigel told me that he was planning to get married on 18th December, 2010. This was great news for all of us. I was very excited for him. We had lots of planning to do throughout the year. I let all my families know. I was happy when Sanjay and family told me they definitely would come over from Canada. My sister too was joining them. This was a time when all the families could get together. They wanted their children to meet all the cousins, aunties and uncles in Australia. My sister Roshni from New Zealand also told me she would not miss Nigel's wedding for anything. Sure enough she came with her whole family. This was so encouraging for me to have all the support from my families. It was only March now and already I felt the mood of the wedding in my heart. As I talked to my families locally, they were all very excited to be coming over to Brisbane; this is where the wedding was taking place. I booked the motels for all of us going over. Nigel's cousins were coming from interstate. His work mates all planned to there, so did his best friends from school days. All my brothers, sisters and their families gave me their names for the accommodation. Sure enough I booked three different motels since there were many visitors coming. It made no difference to anyone even if the wedding was in Brisbane they all decided to be there for us. This was an expensive trip for everyone.  Thank you all for your support!

When I visited my specialist, he told me the surgery on my foot could be 'anytime'. Now I wasn't sure if "anytime" actually meant anytime. I waited all the year but now it came close to this wedding time. I told Nigel "if I'm not at your wedding I'm really sorry but this surgery is more important to me." By now my foot had become really out of shape. I had to walk with a walking stick.  Month after month I waited while preparing for the wedding.

I had shattered bones in my left foot for ten years but I didn't know about this until four years ago. From time to time I had this painful foot. The doctors gave me cortisone injections which made it feel a little better. I did this for very long time. One day my specialist asked me if I had any X-rays done on this foot. I didn't. He organized one for me with an ultrasound too. When the results came, we were shocked. Even the person doing the ultrasound asked if I'd ever had a brick fall on my foot. I said I hadn't, but then I told her that in January 2000 when my husband passed away, my daughter collapsed and fell on my foot, her knee hit my foot. At that time my foot was very swollen. This pain was nothing compared to the pain of losing my husband. I didn't do anything about it. Some months later the pain came back. This went on for some time so I took it very lightly. In the recent months, however, the pain had become worse. I noticed that the shape of my foot was becoming more crooked. I haven't worn a normal pair of shoes for years. My foot went flat, so there was no curve on my left foot.

It was only after my specialist saw that was such a bad problem that I decided to have the surgery. While waiting for it to be done, I went to have acupuncture to relieve the pain. The pain was worse day by day. I couldn't balance myself properly. I continued balancing myself with walking stick for weeks, then months. Previously I had a major surgery on my spine. My back had been really good all these years but the it recurred. I waited to hear from the hospital desperately.

I kept asking God for wisdom and the right timing for my foot operation. The doctors told me that after surgery I wouldn't be able to put my foot on the floor for six weeks. Then I would slowly walk on my heels. I would have to go through physiotherapy for eight to nine months before I could walk properly." This was a year out of my calendar. What would happen to the wedding in all of this?

I informed all my families coming for the wedding about the surgery so it wouldn't be a big shock to them when they arrive. They all also prayed for everything. This all-knowing God had other plans for me. He definitely knew the desire of my heart. Just a week before the wedding, I rang the hospital to ask about the surgery. They told me there were no surgeries done from December to February. I was so excited! At last I knew I would be there for the wedding! Hurray! "Even if I was in pain" Thanks be to God!

How could I not be at my son's wedding? Is God so bad that He didn't see the desire in my heart to be there? The all-knowing God knew Nigel didn't have a dac, how would He not look after me to be there? I'm the mum and dad for him. How wonderful that God works everything for good for those who love Him dearly (Rom 8:28)! Praise God, I was there and even if I had my walking stick, I saw my son's wedding. I'm so grateful I had the support of all my families from near and far. We had the most wonderful wedding for my son. God blessed us with good weather for this occasion.

The owner of this function centre told me that for a whole month they had not seen any sunset. The weather had been miserable and cloudy. On this day God sent a beautiful sunset so we all took pictures of the beauty of God's creation from the mountain top. The lady too was in awe to see at last the sunset. Just two days after a great time at the wedding we saw the biggest flood that I have ever seen in my entire life. I Praised God that He held on to this rain and flood until the wedding was over.

*"Bundle of joy"*
*Zachariah*
*29th, October 2010*

While Nigel and Shazza went on their honeymoon to Borneo, all our families travelled back from Brisbane to our place in Sydney for Christmas and New Year 2011. For all the cousins, this was the time of their lives! We had so much fun and fellowship with all the families with us in Sydney. Some families we hadn't seen for up to fifteen years. This was such a great festivity to celebrate with one another—it was really a family re-union in some ways. It was great that the cousins were able to get bonded as many hadn't even met all these years. We certainly had a wonderful time together. While enjoying ourselves, it always brought back memories of Patrick not being with us. Our lives are gifts from God.

Nige and Shaz were married for only three months when I had to move in with them for my recovery time.  Since I was on wheelchair for a while it was really convenient staying at Nigel and Shazza's place. God in His grace gave them a home that had a ramp for my wheelchair. They took such wonderful care of me as I watched them grow in love. I really appreciated the love and care given to me during my eight weeks with them.

As I look at all my children I can see Patrick in them clearly. With him in my heart and him watching us from on high, I am happy to keep going for the Lord with my children. When anyone sees my children, they say, "He is Patrick all over again!" All of them have Patrick's great qualities. This constantly reminds me of him. Hazel has teaching abilities like her dad and some of his comedian ways.  Nigel is mature, compassionate as well as sensible.  He gets very excited about things, has a great heart, of course he also has a heart problem like his dad. Regi has got his dad's playful, comedian side and is very intelligent like dad.  How does God do all these things in our lives? Can I ever get away from Patrick? God has been my wonderful and faithful partner all this time.

In my little Zac, my grandson, as he is growing day by day I see great qualities of a musician in him. Surely as he grows older we will see more of his character from his grandfather. Every time I look after him, we play music. He knows how to play in the right rhythm, plays the shaker, drum, tambourine and dances along as well. It's great that even the next generation has a little of my lovely husband's characteristics. I will never get tired of watching all these 'Patrick's in action.  Patrick has multiplied in many of us. Even Lian in Burma has named his two children after my family, his daughter is Hazel and his son is Patrick. He too is waiting to see his 'little Patrick' in action like our Patrick was, a man full of action and fun. Thank God for what He is doing in these lives today.

*Zachariah,*
*2 years, 2012*

# 12    Reginel's Health Scare

While we were still celebrating with our many visitors from oversees who were here for the wedding, we got a big shock when Regi, was admitted to hospital with a stroke. We couldn't believe this had happened so quickly. All our celebration turned into sadness.  All the eating these cousins did was probably the cause of the stroke. They all had late nights and eating competitions with bananas, McDonald's, pizzas and Kentucky Fried Chicken to see who could eat the most. Of course, Reg won most of these competitions.

You can imagine how all the cousins cried as they saw Reg in hospital. He was treating it all as a joke, later he got really scared when the doctors couldn't find the cause of his illness in such a young person. They never had a case like this before. They kept him in for several days. As he got better, he ended up playing with his cousins in the hospital courtyard before they left for their homes. After many tests, it was discovered Reg had a clot in the brain which caused this stroke. It was only a temporary thing but it really made him think seriously about his life. He could have died but God has given him another chance in life.

He changed his lifestyle dramatically. He has been on very strict diet. God surely didn't make a mistake as I believe nothing in our lives happens by chance. It is written in Jeremiah 29:11, God knows the plans He has for us. He knew the plans he had for Regi at this time too. Thank God for His amazing knowledge of us.

 Reg had another scan a month later. What happened was amazing!

"My church friends prayed for me and I feel better now," he told the neurosurgeon.

She shook her head and said, "Do you think that will help?"

Reg said, "Yes." This was wonderful for Reg to testify that prayer does work.

Two months later, after another scan, he went to see this same specialist. This time there was not a scar on his brain. The neurosurgeon then looked surprised. "There is no trace of the scar in the brain," she told Reg. "I don't understand it." I believe that God had done this miracle in Reg.

This was God teaching her too that He is in control. How amazing it all was.  Thank you, Lord, for another answered prayer—God you are amazing!

Many times in life we don't even think whether we will really be alive tomorrow. For Reg this was a wake-up call. I was really scared that I lost him forever but thank God He has kept him here for a reason.

Regi has been a brilliant student all through his school days. He came first in all his classes. He seemed to be born with a 'big brain.' He was a bookworm like his father. They both had a great relationship. When Patrick passed away, he gave up everything. His studies went downhill. I kept encouraging him, but he had given up everything in life for a very long time. He carried a lot of pain in his heart. He never shared this with us.

He always said to me, "Mum, you have many burdens to carry for us all. Let me carry my burdens myself. I don't want you to worry about me. You are very sick yourself, I don't want you to die as well, I'd rather not burden you anymore." Little did he know that it hurt me more to see him in difficult situations!  As the years went by, he picked up, always studying at the last minute. Now after all these years he has gone through University and finished with a Bachelor's degree in Business and Commerce (Applied Finance). I'm so proud of him. Even if it did take longer to finish his studies, he did finally graduate. He is working for a bank in the city.. I thank God for helping him through all the difficult days without his dad.

With God all things are possible. I believe one day he'll be able to witness to others what God has done in his life as well as use his experience to help others. He has matured lots and I am amazed at the way he has cared for me through the time I had my second surgery. In every detail he understood me in my pain. He even did cooking, cleaning, washing and all the housework. God has been teaching him and me lots of things that we have done together.

There is another side of Reg.  He was always accident prone. Just when we got to Australia Reg, Nige and cousin Sam were playing in Sam's garage.  We were all busy in the kitchen cooking.  Suddenly I saw Reg go to the laundry. Sam went in the house to grab a band-aid. I ran after them asking what had really happened. While playing Regi hit the corner of this fridge. This was a old rusty fridge. He was bleeding profusely as he had a very deep cut in his upper arm. The boys decided they won't tell us adults that's why Sam came in for the band-aid. Amazing idea! Little brains thinking they can get away with this! We had to rush Reg to hospital and he had the wound stitched up.

Another of his accidents was like this: He left home for a soccer match.  They played really well as this was their final match. Just an hour after he left home I had a call from his friend "Mrs Datta, can you come to hospital, Reg had a bit of an accident at soccer." I rushed in to see him. I couldn't believe this was Regi.  I didn't know whether to laugh or cry. Within just few minutes, Reg had a very square face. His jaw was hanging down so low I had never seen anything like this. His face was really swollen badly.  I had to take him to another hospital to have this emergency surgery which took 4 hours. He had inside his mouth plates, wires, bands and metals he was not allowed to eat any food. For six weeks I fed him through straws.  Every hour I had to cook, mash everything and make gravy in all the food, so he could swallow his food in with a straw. This was a busy time for me.  I was on the go all the time, just finding new things to feed him!

Like me, Regi has had lots of pins, plates and screws in his body. He had a nose surgery, mouth and jaw repaired and his broken foot fixed, then the worst was the stroke.
His hobbies are to travel the world and he travelled 22 countries in Europe in the last 9 weeks. He loves music, parties and being a DJ at functions.

I was really blessed by him on Valentine's Day.  He woke up early, made me lovely breakfast in bed with pikelets, muffins, bacon and egg. With a rose in his hand he got all these to my bed, what a surprise that was! I wanted to cry.  This was Patrick all over again in him. Things like these really touch my heart.

For Father's Day at 8am this email came from Europe:

*"Hey mum, Happy father's day! Hope you have an awesome day and hope the family spoil you! Thanks for being both mum and dad for all these years!"*

*"I'll see you next week"* Reggie

Isn't that such a lovely gesture? I love the words he has written.  He knows that all these years have been tough for me but I was there for all of them. Hazel and Nigel have done these things in all the past years but Reg made sure he sent a message first while so far away. I thank God that life has changed heaps for him.  I love the way he goes to work in his suit and tie.  He has really come a long way. Both of us enjoy our time together in this beautiful place God has blessed us with.  One day it's my desire to see him settle down and have a family of his own. Praying that I am here to see this happen, God willing!  In all things I love God to have His way in my life. This life He has given me is for a great purpose, "Not my will but yours be done!"

Lian & the Children
Myanmar Hostel

# 13  The Work in Myanmar (Burma)

GLO has been a major part of our lives for many years. They have worked with many countries around the world including Fiji.  In the Gospel Schools where we worked for many years, they came to help in the building projects. When we served GLO for 12 months, we admired the faith of all the leaders. They continued to pray daily for all their workers. They are the most godly people I have worked with. I am very grateful for their impact in my own life. I know how prayer is powerful as God opens doors through prayers.

At one of GLO's celebration dinner we met a very quiet, gentle and humble looking person. Patrick is one who sees a person like Lian, he must provoke him so he can talk. He had his "style" to "bring the person out of his shell." You wouldn't believe this but Lian got a shock when Patrick said "hello, nice to meet you" and next he started punching his stomach in a joke. Lian told me later. "I have never seen a man like Him. I thought he must be mentally sick or what." Would you ever do that to any new person? No, Patrick had his unique weird ways. That's his first meeting!

GLO leaders had met Lian (from Myanmar) in Malaysia for the first time. They got him over to study with their program in Riverstone, Sydney. After this  he was given an opportunity to study at GLO Smithton, in Tasmania.

When Lian joined us at this Bible College Patrick and Lian became the best of friends. They poured out  their heart and prayed together for the future of the work in Myanmar. They cried their hearts to God for wisdom and help.  They would have given their lives for each other! Their friendship was like David  and Jonathan, the story from 1st Kings in the Bible. They knew each other's  heart, mind and soul. One of their prayers was for starting work in Myanmar.  They shared the vision of reaching people for Christ.

Their friendship was like David and Jonathon from the story of 1 Kings  n the Bible. They knew each other's 'heart, mind, soul' they cried to God together. One of their prayers was for starting work in Myanmar. They felt each other's pain. They also shared the vision of reaching people for Christ.

When Lian told us about how he wanted to start work in Myanmar, we did everything to help. There was great persecution for Christians in his land. What the people needed was Christ. Only Lian knew how difficult it would be to share the Gospel to the poor and neglected people. We all got praying before he was to return to Burma.  Pat got our church members, Eastwood church friends, GLO friends, our families, all together we raised funds for his work. Praise God, He provided enough money. Lian started with 8 children and helped them in every way possible.

This was the start of something only God could do. He provided the GLO family to take care of Lian's work in Myanmar. Now after 13 years, amazing things have happened. God has blessed them with many children who have come to find Jesus in their lives.  The work has grown physically and spiritually through the work that Lian, his brother Kot and all their families are doing together.

When Patrick was serving in Belmore he told Lian we were a hundred percent behind his ministry in Burma. "We will support you not only in prayer, but financially as well. Whatever you need, we will look after you and your work," Pat told him. This we did for a little while.

After Patrick passed away, Lian was very disturbed he had lost his great friend and brother. We had promised to support him financially in his work. In the meantime, I had been thinking a lot about them and wrote Lian a letter. God had put the words of **Joshua 1:1-9** in my heart. The Lord tells Joshua, **"Moses is dead and now you, Joshua have to take over the job and lead the people into the Promised Land."** I had to apply these verses to Lian and me in this work as well.

"Now Patrick is dead, Lian," I wrote, "you and I will have to carry on the work, you with your people in Myanmar and I with the people here, that God has given me to take care;  to lead them to the Lord. This work does not belong to Patrick, me or you, Lian. It's His work—we are only His servants and the instruments He is using. Please do not give up. As far as support is concerned, God will provide. As he has in the past, so He will in the future. We need to trust Him and have faith that He will do all good things for us."

Even though times were tough, God used this letter to encourage them all to "never give up." God will definitely supply their needs. Today the work there is blooming in every sense. Many more under-privileged children now have Jesus in their lives. They serve the Lord in different parts of Burma. What a wonderful and powerful God we have!

GLO Ministries have been there all the way.  There's always someone there helping in the hostels, lands, farm work and financially helping them throughout all these years. They brought many of the children to train them for future ministry of Myanmar. Students like Kot, Naing, Nunu, Kaikai who are already helping in the work there. Hazel is studying now to join Lian in this ministry. Many people from GLO families have visited them and financially supported them. They have done such a wonderful job on the farms they have bought in the recent years. This farm now produces lots of food for the whole hostel children. They are able to sell some things as well.  Truly our God is an all-knowing God and I praise God that many lives have been changed for eternity. May God richly bless all who have been behind this great work of God!

When I went to visit them in December 2006/ January 2007, I was amazed at the children. They had two hundred altogether in the hostel. By this time, GLO had bought more homes for the children. There were two hostels for girls and one for boys. God definitely has provided, with GLO ministries, we've been able to achieve great things in this nation. Many who are believers were baptized. They have finished their studies as well as graduated from universities. Some have grown up there in the hostel and are back to serve the children as teachers and leaders.

These children have grown spiritually as well as physically. Some of them are in primary school, others in high school. Last year the children's results at school were outstanding. Every child did very well in school. This is the result of the hard work of the leaders. Every day they have leaders who take time to teach them at home. Even the school principal was amazed at the great results of the children. When their soccer teams play against other teams in the community they notice what wonderful boys they are. These leaders of the community have great respect for Lian and the outstanding task that he has undertaken in training these boys.

In the last thirteen years, many children have come and gone. We thank God they came to know Jesus as their Saviour.  They recite the Bible fluently. They know how to live their lives in Christ wherever they go. Some have left to do mission work among their own tribal people. God's work is expanding. I thank God that the work now has been such a blessing to the community and families too.

If the children were not at the hostel, they would have died of hunger. Their testimonies are truly amazing. These children are very talented—some in singing, drama or art and some in teaching and being leaders. Some of them are kitchen hands and cooks. During my last two trips, I met all the children. I spent time working with them, helping them wherever I could. They are truly an amazing bunch of children, content and happy in whatever little they own there at the hostel. It's no exaggeration, but some children own only one or two sets of clothes plus a blanket for their bed. This is where we have come in—to help get things for them. Praise God He has blessed us so we can bless others.

My two trips to Myanmar was a great learning process. I prepared the Christmas dinner and New Year dinner for them. On the seventh and the tenth anniversary of my husband's passing, I cooked for more than three hundred guests. They were grateful for every little thing I did. Many things we throw away in our country they would gladly keep as a treasure. Life in that part of the world is really difficult.

Every one of the children really worked hard on the little garden they have. It was fascinating to see what a blessing all their crops are on the farm. The garden in front of the hostel was green, lush and healthy. It feels like God has a special blessing in their gardens. I believe God has been providing them with food through everything they planted—the fruits of their own hard work. We praise God that from their farm, they are able to provide enough crops, for the children. Great is thy faithfulness, O God my Father!

Please pray for my dear friends and children who live there. Lian and his whole family have dedicated their lives to serving these poor children. Even though they as a family are so poor, they share whatever they have with these children. When they don't have anything, they all pray together.  God mysteriously provides them with food. Praise God for this great ministry! Today you are reaping the harvest with so many more children there.

I see this work as a great mission field for training young people, not only with knowledge but with physical food first then the spiritual food. They all have good spiritual food daily. They all learn, memorize many verses and recite them to others when they get together. It's like a great competition but these words will not return unto the Lord empty. It will reap one day and bring forth a harvest of fruit in His work in Burma. I believe many more will go out to preach and teach others what they have learnt in their lives. This will truly be a missionary sending hostel. We give all glory to our God who answers prayers.

**Our "Dreams of a Hostel"**

Many years ago when my mum in law was with us, she shared her desire to have a hostel to take care of homeless and under-privileged children. All her life she took care of many of these people. When she passed away, Patrick and I had the same desire to have a hostel where Patrick could look after the spiritual side and I would be the cook and caretaker. Two years after my mum in law passed away, Patrick too passed away. I knew I can't do such a job on my own. God in His wisdom gave me all these children at this hostel that I can be part of them, in caring, praying, providing in whatever little I am able to do. How good is God? He fulfilled our hearts' desires—first mum's, then Pat's and now mine too.

*Mark & Nani Kushma, 2001*

MARK (7yrs) drew for my Birthday

Thank you Nani, (grandma) for all the lovely things we are able to do together. Every sleepover we had at your place, Daemion and I enjoyed the best time; we could play video games, go to park to play and watch movies at your home. School holidays were the best when we could go out to movies, and watch lovely children's movies. We loved eating out, buying things plus having lots of fun with you. My favourite was bubble bath time. You bought us many gifts we enjoyed all our lives. Thank you for cooking our favourite food and looking after us so much all the time. Nani, we pray for you every day. Love you, Nani!

**Mark and Daemion Tin
(grand children)**
Students Primary School
Sydney Australia

*A Tribute to queen Nani
Drawn by Mark 7 years old.*

# 14  My Soul Restored

When we first came to minister at Belmore Church in 1998, we met many people from all different countries. We also worked with Dr GD James, as he always invited us to many of his meetings. In one of his meetings we met a girl named Deborah. She came from Burma. She was very talented in music. She was searching for a church where she would fit in to worship and be used of God. She was in this country to study music while her husband stayed back in Singapore to work. Deborah had also studied at the Singapore Bible College. In one of Dr James meetings, Patrick introduced himself to her. Pat asked her to come and sing in our church one day. Shortly after, she came and met all our young people from all nationalities. She decided to join our church as she felt really comfortable with all the different types of people. They all spent lots of time in our home, having meals and fellowship with us regularly.

We had a huge family of Pakistani, Filipino, Korean, Burmese, Chinese and of course our own Indian children. We all served the Lord together as we all grew through Bible studies. Everyone worked hard in church too. This also reminded me of the believers in the book of Acts when all the people ate together, studied God's Word and served the Lord with all their hearts and minds. We organized trips to the city and Zoo, Harbour Bridge walk, putt putt golf and many other places. God definitely blessed all the children growing together in Christ. Many went through lots of troubles and difficulties with immigration. With God's help we stuck together to help in every way possible. Pat and I had one aim - to minister to them in their need.

I'm so thankful to God for all our adopted children. Wilson Masih, now married with 2 children is leaving to serve God as a missionary in Pakistan.  He is serving with GLO Ministries. When he arrived in Australia many years ago, he was frightened, worried, insecure and in a lot of pain, emotionally and physically. God has truly changed his life and what a blessing to see him go back to his own country to serve his own people. Together with Wilson we had Sohail and Sam. Today Sohail is a pastor, taking care of God's flock in Pakistan. As for Sam, he leads his church with his family too. I'm grateful to God that all we invested in their lives has been worth it. They are all serving God in Pakistan. What a blessing!  We all are His servants together doing His work in different parts of the world.

As for Deborah, she has been a most faithful friend and a very special daughter to me. The first day she met all these young people who called me "Mum", Deb said, "Can I also please call you mum?"  I said, "Of course you can." Some of the children had no families in this strange land. God gave this job to me to use it for His glory. They needed a family and our home was open to all. Many have now returned to their homes. Some serve the Lord in their churches.  Others found Christ here and are still walking with the Lord. I give thanks to God for their time with us. Deborah has stayed with us for the last fourteen years.

While Deb did music every Sunday morning in church, Paul was the technician. After a few years in our church their first child was born. I loved him as this kept me busy taking care of his needs while Deb and Paul kept the music side going. That was a special time for me to see this little baby grow in front of my eyes. Now he is almost twelve years old. We prayed for every little difficulty baby Mark went through. When he started talking, he would say out of nowhere, "Nani (grandma), I love you, Nani!" It made me cry many times as that was the year my husband passed away.

I needed that closeness, the comfort of being loved. He was really close to my heart. He would run to me as soon as he saw me in church and jump on to my lap.  I felt so much needed as well as loved, beyond my imagination.

Those thoughtful words that came out of little Mark, my grandson was no coincidence, it was as if God used him to care for me, loving me so deeply. Who would say "I love you" just when I needed to hear this? When I was going through difficult days or was sick, my little boy Mark would encourage me. He was truly an angel sent by God to be by my side just at the time when Patrick wasn't there. I felt God's timing was amazing. God knew my needs, He understood me, saw my pain and my deepest sorrows.  Here was God's angel with so much love to share with me. He would say things like "Nani, I want to help you do the dishes." He was only so small—maybe two years old then — he would climb on a chair to help. He distracted me from missing my husband. He involved me in Mark's life. How great is our God! Deborah was really new to this country. I was a mum to her as she was a wonderful daughter to me.

Every Sunday after church we, families got together—my brother's family, my sister's family along with any new members who came to church. I loved having everyone over for fellowship. Deborah and Paul were our most faithful company. Mark would always want to come home with me as I went to prepare for our lunch times. Deb would join us for lunch when she finished sorting out the music. These lunch times were a gathering of many saints from different parts of the world who were visiting us in church. Some folks had just arrived as migrants and some were new students who have come to study at one of the universities in Sydney. I felt these gatherings united us to serve God, strengthen our spiritual lives as well as helped us all work together.

Mark was the only baby in church. Everyone loved him and cared for him. He was no problem in church. From the beginning he sat with me quietly and happily. As he grew bigger, he would do his colouring. I made sure I had enough pens as well as paper for his weekly drawing. He drew pictures so brilliantly. I was amazed at how gifted he was. Even in his young age he received a prize for his drawing from the Epping Community Fair.

One Sunday, I couldn't go to church. I was sick for the whole week with my back problem. Mark came and saw me sick in bed as I couldn't move. Normally I would feed him every time he was around. This time he told everyone, "I'm having lunch with Nani on her bed."

After lunch, I couldn't believe what I heard.

"Nani, can I sing a song to you?" he asked.

 "Of course darling," I said.

Then he sang this song which was like a sermon from a pastor:

"Jesus, you're my firm foundation, I know I can stand secure.
Jesus, you're my firm foundation, I put my hope in your holy Word….
"Your Word is faithful, mighty in Power.., God will deliver me of this I'm sure…"

I didn't know the correct words of this song as I had never heard it before. I asked Deb for the words. I told her what the little "pastor" had done in my spiritual life.

76

I had been alone all week. I was missing my husband in this time of sickness. Hazel was now preparing to get married. Life was changing fast for me. By the end of the week, I felt so alone and discouraged in my soul. When Mark sang this song for me, it went over and over in my mind, convicting me of God's sure love. I was so overwhelmed—these were the words that ministered to me in the coming weeks. This was what helped me to keep my eyes focused on my Lord. I couldn't understand how a child like Mark, being only three years old, could bring such a powerful word from God to me at the right time. No wonder we have in the Bible that 'from the mouth of babes will come the praises of God.'

Since I really loved this song, I asked Mark if he could sing this on Hazel's wedding. All eyes were on Him as he opened his mouth! There was pin drop silence. The applause he got after went on and on! This was truly amazing, the highlight of my day!

My life with the grandchildren has been very interesting, a learning process too. As a widow I felt dead within myself. Those hugs, the closeness and affection in my life were gone too. My children were grown up teens, they would hug me from time to time. They were struggling as well.  However, it was different when the little baby came in the picture. Ten months after Patrick died, Mark was born. He has been like an angel in my life. His presence comforted my children as they loved playing with him. God used this little child to calm my spirit, renewing my life for His service. I was blessed from Mark's real deep love for me, his 'Nani' (grandma).

Deborah loved our special food "dhal" which is Indian lentils. When we first started feeding him solids food,  he preferred dhal to anything for Sunday lunch. As a very little boy, he came to sleep over at my place. We all had lovely times doing many interesting baby things. We went out to the parks and hung out in the sun. I would bring him home to give him a bubble bath. Bubble bath was always the highlight for him!

When Deborah went into labour with Daemion, Mark stayed with me through the night.  Late at night he was sobbing, when I heard him I started crying as this was the first time he cried while at our place. I asked him "what happened darling?" He wanted to see mummy. Early next morning I took him over to see mum in hospital. He was really happy to see mummy. He turned around, there was a new baby Daemion, he reacted funny and turned away.

Mark's funny reaction reminded me of Hazel, when she was the only child in my family. The day I got Nigel from hospital to our place she was angry and took off. All day she played with her friends and didn't even come home for meals. I was really busy so later I thought "I haven't seen Haze for a while" then went out to get her.  She told me "I'm not coming home anymore as you have another baby, and you all don't love me anymore" I was stunned and hugged her. I had to explain how important a part she had in taking care of this new baby brother. Since then she helped me with the nappy change, passing all the little things to me. I really was shocked to see her reaction.

Daemion was totally different from Mark. He loves his food at any time. Mark really loves and cares for his little brother. Mum and dad have taught them many memory verses. I love the way both of them recite the verses in church. One day I believe God will use them both for His work. They are the leaders of the next generation. The two boys and I have been praying in church every Sunday. Their prayers were so innocent but genuine. I could see both of them grow right in front of my eyes and now they are using their gifts for God. Praise God for their lives.

In recent times, they sing as a family, in our church, in the Burmese fellowship meetings and at camps. They all are very dedicated to music. Paul plays drums while Deb plays the piano or organ.  Now my little Mark is big enough to play the keyboard in our worship service. Our church in Belmore really appreciates all the work Deborah has put into our music. This has lifted the spirit of worship in our church.  Daemion has played the tambourine also a little drum as he continues to learn to play drum for future.  How great it is for me to see these children are used by God in their early life.

When Daemion was born, I continued caring for both the boys. I kept them occupied during church time. They were really good boys. Mark did all his drawings and Kumo (maths). Damien was interested in something to eat. He loves his food! I made sure I had enough snacks for the entire service.

Once when his real grandma (from Myanmar) came to look after them, she rang me early in the morning. I thought someone must be sick. She told me Mark doesn't listen to anyone except you the "Nani"

"Can you please talk to Mark?" she asked. "He doesn't want to go to school."

I asked him why he didn't want to go to school.

"My teacher gets angry when I can't do my Maths," he told me.

"Let's tell God about it," I said. "He knows how to help."

We prayed for this problem, and today, praise God, Mark is really good in Maths. He even received awards from school and Kumo (maths) School. We prayed to God for little and big things. God answered even this little prayer. **God is able to give to us exceedingly abundantly more than we ask or even imagine (Eph 3:20).**

It has been good for the boys to know (like my own children) that God is there to help us in my need anytime. Now Mark does a great job of reading the Bible in church. He sings all the hymns and songs. Mark has a great talent of singing like mum. Thank God Daemion is learning lots from his brother.

Both Deb and I had the same mind to spend time in prayer every weekday. We didn't realize as we continued this for almost six years. This was very important for our church growth, for student's schooling, all the activities, our children's future partners and lots more things we prayed. Our prayers got answered one by one. Paul joined Deborah in Sydney then got a job, Permanent Residence and continued to serve the Lord in many different ways. Not forgetting the birth of these beautiful boys in the right time.

There were some weird things we prayed for.  Do you think this was a stupid prayer? No, it wasn't, as God wants us to bring every situation we go through to Him. We were so amazed that within a few days, the problems were solved.  When Deborah started full-time job, we could not have this anymore except when she was free to talk and we ended with prayers.

Deborah has definitely been one of the most faithful daughters I have in the Lord. Her spiritual life and dedication are truly amazing. I praise God for her life, all her musical talents using it all for God's Glory. Today she takes many of the young adults under her 'wings' mentoring and having Bible Studies with them. She really is a great encourager. Since Paul came he works together as a humble servant of our Lord. His nature too is incredible. He is a silent and quiet worker behind the scenes. I am so grateful for him and his love for the Lord. He is a great father to his children too. We praise God for such a godly couple.

My trip to Burma with Debra and family was a great blessing. I met lovely people in Paul and Deborah's family. They love God and are wonderful people. I had my husband's 7th memorial service at Lian's hostel. Many of Debra's family joined us. The boys would not leave me they sat with me and asked me to feed them as usual. The Burmese people were overwhelmed as to how I, an Indian person, was so closely attached to the two Burmese boys. It has been a story that started from their birth and will continue on.

The funny thing about these children is that they would fight over who's going to talk to "nani" on the phone first. When Daemion started talking he wanted to be first. Well Mark was so used to be the only one talking to "nani" but now he had to share that with Daemion.
I rang from Canada to talk to the boys one day.  We had a good conversation. As soon as Mark came on the phone, he said "Nani, nani, Daemion pushed me today in church." To console him I had to say "when I'm back I'll talk to him ok." He had no idea how far away I was. Later talking to Deb I told what he said. She didn't know when this happened, "can't believe he tells you to get all the sympathy."  They are really cute!

Knowing Mark almost twelve years, and Daemion eight years, their love continues for me. As I enter into Church their eyes are full of excitement. By chance if Mark didn't see me, Daemion will tell him "hey Nani is here" oh how cute!

I gave a little of my love and time to Mark as he was growing up. In return Mark has done wonders in my life. It was such perfect timing that God sent this child to minister to me in Patrick's absence. Daemion came as a bonus. How great is our God? Doesn't He plan everything well in our lives? Especially for me!

Deborah and Paul have been very generous in sharing their wonderful children with our family. I have been greatly blessed. Thank you both for all your kindness!  A true Christian spirit!

*Deborah, Paul,
Daemion, Mark*

*Happy faces at the Nursing Home*

*Kushma and Entertainers*
*Eun Ha (left) - Reena (right)*

# 15  Nursing Home Ministry

All my life I knew I was the Pastor's wife. I loved serving the Lord together with Pat. Suddenly I didn't know what my place was in church. With all my heart I wanted to continue serving God. This was my life. I didn't want to sit at home and feel sorry for myself.  All our church friends were very supportive. They encouraged me lots to carry on whatever plans we had for our youth as well as the whole church. I thank God for helping me through this time. This ministry continued as we did not have any Pastor for a long while.

One day I went out to visit two sisters who lived nearby. They came to our church for years. Now they were quite elderly and sick. Both had a beautiful home each. Their homes were filled with the memories of their husbands as well as other loved ones. They shared many stories of their past—all they had done, the places they had visited plus the good experiences with their husbands.

One thing I noticed was that they had many health problems. One sister was deaf, had heart problems while the other sister had a knee replacement, a hip replacement plus many other problems with her foot. Their lives carried on as normal people. They lived on their own. I was very encouraged by them when I realized that I had three children with me. I have God on my side. My church family has always been there for us. I couldn't stay home, mourn and grieve every day.  I must do something for others. This would keep my life going in the right direction. This had to be God! He really opened my eyes to do something for the senior citizens of our church. We had many seniors in our church (maybe half the church was elderly). They needed help all the time.  When I helped them I found some of them lived in nursing homes. This led me to help my community, as they were the neglected people of our land.

I visited them in their different homes cooking meals for them. I took some of them to doctors or any other place they needed to go. I volunteered to pick them up for church and drop them back home. I took them home for meals. I helped them do shopping. I felt really happy seeing them week by week. I could see them going down in their health. Finally they were gone into God's presence. One by one seeing them go made me realize how precious each life is.

One day my friend from church took us to visit a patient in a Retirement Village. This young person was living there for seventeen years that time we saw him. In his motor accident his spine was badly damaged. He has been on wheelchair ever since. Reena is a singer, she was with us. When we sang for him, he started singing with us. He was so overwhelmed. Eventhough we did not understand all his words, his voice was beautiful.

He was really happy as his heart connected with the music. We were amazed that he enjoyed our company. He smiled, laughed with us, held our hands so we could stay longer with him. It was very touching for me to see a young man in a wheelchair for all this time. One accident and his life cut was short. What a life? He was definitely bored sitting there so we made a difference to him.

That very day the Activity Coordinator asked me if we could go back one day and sing for the whole crowd in their Retirement Village. I grabbed this opportunity! This was the beginning of a great work for God. We had a chance to share the gospel. Many lonely people were helped in their own lives. They just wanted to talk as they were very lonely. Some of them were such lovely singers. Among them was a blind lady named Ella and her voice was amazing. Everytime we went back there, we would ask Ella to sing with us. She felt really happy leading us in singing for the crowd.

We started this ministry in February 2006. We visited many nursing homes, retirement homes, hostels, hospitals, churches and senior members' homes for special occasions like birthdays or anniversaries. We have been to individual homes too having Worship plus communion service. These two couples were members of our church for years. Unfortunately the four of them had many health issues. We visited them regularly as they couldn't now get to church. Our four friends got others as well, so we could have a communion service in their home. We had a lovely time singing famous hymns and choruses. They were overjoyed about the afternoon we spent with them. This communion time was the highlight for them. They really appreciated our time together.

Every nursing home we have been to love singing time. Sometimes patients were very sick, they would be in their beds or wheelchairs and in a lot of pain. I shared some of my own experiences such as the sudden death of my husband and what it has taught me. On certain occasions I would share about Mothers' Day, Father's Day, Anzac Day, Easter, Christmas, sharing God's love for us all and how God also has a place for us in Heaven.
This ministry has taught me lots in my own life. Life is very short. Many times we would meet a lovely person and have a good time with them. Next visit she would be gone. It hurt us deeply losing them as friends.

Two of these nursing homes wanted us every month. We celebrated all the birthdays of residents at the end of each month. We all shared cakes with them. I felt really special being there with them to celebrate. Every Easter we visited many of these places.  This was a good time to share what the true meaning of Easter was. Surprisingly some of them went to church or Sunday schools and learnt of Jesus' death and resurrection. Many sang with us as they knew songs from Sunday school days.

In some places we were not allowed to share God's Word. Well, I chose to tell them my own life experiences—how this God had taken care of me when I lost my husband. How I looked after three teenage children on my own, how my health was very bad at that stage, how I was living one day at a time only by God's grace and help.

Once we went to Brisbane to visit some of the nursing homes and retirement villages there. We did many home visits as well, singing for those who had difficulty getting out of their homes. I shared God's Word in the Salvation Army ladies fellowship. We sang for hospital patients in the Boonah Hospital. Boonah is a small suburb close to Ipswich in Brisbane. At this hospital we had a lot of fun. The staff dressed up in country style, hats and all. They loved singing the songs together with us and the patients. The funny thing was they all danced around, asking us to dance, it was a bit embarrassing for me. Ruth, my sister-in-law, organized these meetings in Boonah. Her husband Sid, Reena, Ruth and I had a great team here. Sid is also a country singer. Together with Reena we had an excellent time. The staff at the hospital loved their time with us and begged us to go back to cheer them up again.

In one of the nursing homes in Brisbane, one lady spent a lot of her time with us, telling us how her family left her there. She begged us not to leave her. She gave me her address so I could write to her. I did as soon as I got back home to Sydney. My sister in law who visits them regularly, took the letter to her.  She was really excited that someone cared to send her a letter. After a few days she passed away. I felt really sad for her that so quickly she was gone. I felt relieved that I had already sent her a letter as I had promised.

Reena, (my singer) as a young girl sang in the clubs in different parts of the world. Her husband travelled for his job so Reena went along. She spent years singing and learning songs from all parts of the world. The weird thing is that these songs are famous even here in Australia. When she sings her songs, the people just join in. It's great how God brought Reena and me together. Reena is also a widow like me.  We have the same vision to reach out to people by sharing songs. While she sings I get a message from the songs about Christ and his love for us.

When my husband was a minister in our church at Belmore from 1998-2000, we came to know all the members in our church. Many of the believers were Korean. We loved working with them. We also had many different nationalities join us. We all learnt to work together in this beautiful church. One time when I visited Reena, she had some problem with her eye. She needed to go to the city for an eye operation and I offered to take her. This was the beginning of our good, strong relationship. In recent years Eun Ha also has joined us and together we had Bible studies weekly. As we served the Lord we also grew in our Christian life spiritually. In so doing, they learnt English. We grew together and served the Lord together!

Reena taught Eun Ha to play the Chromer harp. This is the main instrument we use and the sound of this is very soothing. A Chromer Harp is a baby version of the harp from Bible times, such as the one David played for King Saul when he became disturbed in his mind.

We have visited many nursing homes in Belmore, Kingsgrove, Lakemba, Bankstown, Narwee, Miranda, Caringbah, Marrickvile, Strathfield and other places. Since the beginning of our ministry we have visited more than 80 nursing homes that I have on record. Not thinking that this will go on for so many years, many of my first visits are not on record. Many times we have been to individual homes too, playing music to those who are housebound. One of our favourite friends was John Coleman who is over 102 years now.  He has been the fittest person I have met at that age, very alert. He has been our longest surviving (65 years) church member around. We loved surprising him in his own house in Belmore on his birthdays. He just loved the time with us.

We never advertised about our work. Only through one nursing home to the other, by word of mouth people came to look for us. They would ring me, to ask if our group can also go to their nursing home, churches, retirement villages and hostels. God kept opening the doors for us.

When we sing in nursing homes, the active members often like to clap. Some like to dance. Eun Ha is responsible for the dance and she does it very graciously. We do action songs so they can join us too. When we see the joy in the hearts of the people, their smiles, we feel what we're doing is priceless. Many remember some famous hymns and children's songs. I ask them how they know these songs. They are excited to tell me, they used to be in a choir or went to Sunday School when they were young.

When they were so active, worked so hard in our country to make a difference in our community, everyone appreciated them. Right now their lives were a big burden to people—to their families and also for the nurses. The workers are there to help.  Even these places are understaffed. It makes it very hard to look after each patient individually. There are many who need a lot of care but how can the staff do all this for one person when forty others are waiting for them too?

The golden rule from God's Word is **Mattew 7:12 "Do to others what you want them to do for you!"** What are we here for? "Is there anything I can do for our folks? Perhaps help in a nursing home, visiting or even helping our neighbours, our own family members? How can we make a difference in their lives to make them comfortable?

Praise the Lord He gave both of us widows Reena and me strength to carry on all these years. Just recently she had an open heart surgery. She is recovering very well.  I had two surgeries on my foot.  God has seen us through all these years. He will continue to help us in this Ministry. Eun Ha has been a great help and many times she has joined us in the past years. Now she has grand children to care for. Whenever she came with us, she played her chromer harp. This year she played the Ocarina, an instrument that originated in Italy and then went to Japan, but praise God it has come into the hands of this Korean sister who plays so beautifully.  There is so much more I could write about this ministry God has opened up for us. We would love people to join us. Many people are hurting. These dear neglected ones are like our "mothers" and "fathers" or even "grandparents". Let us work together for the lonely and neglected precious souls for the Lord.

Sometimes when we have made bookings for nursing home visits, Satan has his plans to spoil things one way or the other. Today, for instance, we had prepared to go over to Yagoona Senior Citizen's Club but suddenly my health wasn't too good. After much prayer, God made me strong enough to spend the time with the seniors at this place. God truly is amazing, as we give ourselves fully to His work. He is watching over His people and protecting us so that His name will be glorified always. I have learnt also to keep praying for every little detail. Difficulties may come our way but we are still prepared to serve the Lord. Not everyone is happy, and the evil one especially does not like it, but God is the One we are serving. Praise God for all these answered prayers.

During my visits to these homes, I was shocked to meet: former nurses, teachers, lawyers, leaders of big corporate companies. Is it only when people are strong and capable that we honour and respect them?  Life is short. This man has been there in the nursing home for 27 years now. We may be the next person there. One accident can change our lives forever. If I'm in there, how would I like to be treated?  All these residents have one story or another to tell. This is one area of my work I really love to continue, God willing. The big smiles, warm hugs and the joy in their hearts make it all worthwhile. There is joy in my soul and happiness in this work. My heart is sorrowful for these neglected people.

When we started the Nursing Home Ministry, I didn't know how long this will go on. Even after all these years I'm not satisfied. We have just covered a tiny ground. There is so much more to cover. Please pray for this important ministry!

*Serving the various needs of the
nursing home community
2006 - 2010*

From left: Reginel, Aaron, Hazel,
Shazza, Nigel, Kushma, 2010

Bali Trip, 2007
Nigel, Hazel, Kushma

# 16  Fullness of Life

## Highlights of my life

I have many highlights in my life. On my fiftieth birthday, my children surprised me by taking me to Bali. We had the best time—all five of us. After my husband passed away, we didn't go anywhere in the school holidays. As he died on one of our holiday trips, it always brought back memories for us all. One by one the years passed. We didn't realize how long it had been since we had a holiday. My children did a great job organizing things. We enjoyed the great adventure in Bali. The food, the culture, the people and the shopping all of us did was extraordinary. It was time to catch up on all those lost years. We did that extravagantly.

God has blessed me with lovely children who made my 50th birthday such an outstanding event. Before we left for our Bali trip, Hazel organized a Hawaiian theme party for all my families as well as my friends in Sydney. That was a big surprise for me. In Bali we did all things together. We stayed in three different hotels. They kept the best hotel for my birthday. That day they took me out on a cruise, dinner and entertainment on the boat. We saw the best sunset ever. We did many funny things like going on a jet ski and other water rides. Can you imagine me on the ski, yes, I went on this but my son deserted me in the middle of the ocean. Just as well I had my life jacket on. We took a tour of an island with many animals, turtles, snakes, birds as well as other sea creatures. We went to the monkey forest. We had great fun with the monkeys. The best thing was while Reg was video shooting these monkeys, they came and snatched his ear piece. We just laughed at how fast they worked!

One of the dares we had for my birthday was a massage for everyone. We had lots of massages to relax. It was really cheap. Aaron was not for massage as he felt someone was intruding his privacy. On my birthday, we all had three hour massage. It was very relaxing for us all. Aaron came out of the massage room. He said "my dignity has gone out the window." Our hotels were lovely, very affordable clean and cheap. My children made sure we had the best hotel for my birthday. Ramada was amazing—the scenery, the food, the architecture inside and out. The restaurant was classy plus the food was outstanding. I just praise God, for my family as well as for this wonderful opportunity to see another part of God's creation. He opened the way for us to have this well deserved holiday.

The Bali trip was planned by God. He used my children to give me a great time. I wouldn't have ever thought of these things. My fiftieth birthday was great, something I will never forget.

One of my dreams in life was to meet Joni Eareckson Tada. The year Patrick passed away, she happened to come over for the Para Olympics in Sydney. She had meetings in different places. My niece Cheryl and I planned to go over to see her. It was like a miracle that this was possible. God even allowed me to take pictures with her. I have her autograph in my Bible that I carry in my handbag every day. What a blessing this was! I was also invited to a luncheon meeting for politicians and church leaders with Joni in the city. How cool was this? **Eph 3: 20 "God is truly able to do exceedingly abundantly more than we imagine or think."** He did this for me!

Why did I have such a desire to see my dear Joni? I hated reading books. My husband gave me this book 30 years ago. That's my first book I read. I was really eager to finish it to see what happened. Her book about the accident and all she went through made me cry. I thought no one had gone through so much pain and suffering besides our Christ. Humanly speaking, she went through lots. Whenever I was down, I would read one of her books. I would feel very encouraged. I managed to read many of her books.

I prayed I would always be godly and shine the light of Jesus like her. This was my prayer for years but sometimes when we do pray, as Joni says, we need to be careful what we pray for, because God will answer and we might regret it. These words are so very true. I always wanted to be like my mum in law and prayed for this. God has given me a little portion of her love and kindness. I try to serve like her in reaching out to the lonely and homeless people. I really try hard to imitate her ways. I didn't ask God to give me my mum in law's sickness. Well, now I do have her problems as well. She was treated for depression at one stage. I did not ask God for that but I did suffer from that after Patrick passed away. It's all under control now. Praise God for the medicine that has helped me, but I am amazed God gave me her sickness as well as little of her good ways.

I prayed to the Lord that I really wanted to be like Joni. I didn't mean that I wanted to be in a wheelchair. (I was in a wheelchair like Joni just for a while). I wanted only the good parts of her life. How selfish of me! Joni only became what she is now because of how she struggled through life. She trusted and believed in God—it was like going through the fire and coming out on the other side, refined and shining like gold. We as God's children have to go through life like that to shine in the end. Going through the process is the difficult thing. None of us ever want to go through that, I'm quite sure. Yet whether we like it or not, God is training us to persevere in these types of circumstances. We all have our share of suffering and trials, but we are also blessed with so many great and wonderful blessings in life too. Our God is a wonderful God.  He cares for us in every area of our lives.

**The trip to USA and Canada**

Everything about this trip was God anointed. Seeing snow fall on the mountains, and experiencing what only God is able to do out of season teaches me to have strong faith in my God all the time.  He can do anything anytime He chooses to do for us who love Him.

*Blue Lagoon Cruise, 1999*
*Enjoying a gentle breeze!*

**Blue Lagoon Cruise**

I went to Fiji to leave my niece who flew to Canada. The next few days I stayed with my sister Roshni who worked for Blue Lagoon Cruises. One morning, she called me from work to ask if I was interested to go on a cruise. It will be for four days and three nights. She called me about 9.30am. I said "I will have to ask my husband." When I called my husband and asked him if I could go. He said "It's up to you if you want to go" I didn't like that tone so I told my sister, maybe next time. I put the phone down but I couldn't think of anything else. I was excited thinking I should go, it will do me good to get away. Then I just prayed. My prayer to God was "Lord, you know my heart, if you want me to go you will make Patrick ring me before time. He will tell me with all his heart that I should go." Just within one hour he rang back saying the most beautiful words, "you have never asked me for anything in life, all this time we have been married, I would love you to go and have a good holiday." The Cruise Ship was leaving at 1 pm. My sister sent me a taxi. I just packed the little I had and left. My husband had paid for everything by phone. Praise God, all went well. Surprise, surprise! My sister booked me into a wonderful luxury honey-moon suite for this trip. This Ship was a new one that had just come in. I could not get over the fact that God had opened the door for me to go. This trip was really a relaxing time for me. I had "me time" and lots of it too. I went snorkelling, I had never done before. The underground corals were magic. I saw the most beautiful coloured fish. What lovely creation of our great God that I really enjoyed. This trip happened just five months before Patrick's passing. This again was as if Pat knew he won't be there for too long so he let me enjoy this time alone with God.

My experience was extraordinary. What a blessing this was. I shared with all my family on my return. Once again my rich family members told me in a very sarcastic way "your God seems to answer you very quickly". My heart sank, "yes I'm happy that God loves me enough to bless me with great things such as the cruise." As a servant of this God, He has truly blessed me more than I have deserved.

**Weird experiences**

One time while the boys were still quite young and Haze was about eighteen, Pat said to me, "Let's go and spend a night at a hotel in Manly?" I told him I wasn't comfortable leaving the children alone. He said Hazel was responsible enough to care for the boys. She did a great job as the boys did enjoy a night alone without the parents. They had a lovely dinner with Hazel. We had some Thai food in Manly. I had never stayed in a hotel (as we couldn't afford this)—and this was the Park Royal Hotel. Since Patrick had accumulated enough points on his Commonwealth Bank credit card, he had a choice of either going free to New Zealand or spending a night in a luxury Park Royal Hotel. He chose the Hotel.

What I couldn't work out was why Patrick chose to have a night in a hotel rather than fly to New Zealand. It was as if Patrick knew he wouldn't be around to go to New Zealand for Regina's, (Pat's niece) wedding that same year (Dec 2000). I was really taken aback as to how this happened. How did Pat know to take the hotel deal rather than the New Zealand trip? This sounds weird, but it's true.

Since the kids managed very well on their own once, Pat then arranged for us to go away again for two nights to Garringong, south of Wollongong. I again hesitated. He was really excited to leave. He went and checked the oil, water plus everything for the car to leave soon. Normally, I would do this job very carefully, but when Patrick gets excited no one can ever stop him. We enjoyed our journey there. When we reached the destination, however, there were fumes coming out of the car. Our host came out and welcomed us. Then he saw that we had a problem in the car. "We'll have to wait for the car to cool down before opening the bonnet to see what had happened inside." When we did open it, you can't even imagine what we saw. Patrick had forgotten to put the cap back on after putting the oil in. The whole engine was covered with the splatter of oil. It was a disaster!

This wasn't a holiday, unfortunately the engine of the car seized. We had to get a tow truck to take it to the mechanic's to be repaired. We returned home after two days with no car, no holiday, but the car problem. We had to put in a new engine and Patrick travelled everyday to Wollongong until the car was fixed.

These two holidays we went by ourselves were just two months before Patrick passed away. What a whole lot of memories! They were holidays I will never forget. It feels like Patrick was rushing to get everything done before leaving me to go to Heaven.

## Singapore/India

My trip with my husband to Singapore was a great experience as well as a highlight. I always felt I have been the blessed one in my family to visit many countries. I learnt a lot about Missions, Evangelism, different cultures, food, lifestyle, language and yet felt God brought us all together as we are all one in Christ. All the amazing things that we saw in India also had been my eye opener. My thoughts were: "what if I were born in that poverty and lay there on one of those streets" yet I was born with God's knowledge. What a blessing!

The lesson for me in both these countries was: God's people live in every part of the world. They made us feel comfortable, provided food, transport also excepting our ministry in their Churches. In Singapore, God even used this lady Caroline to provide my physical need (clothes etc).

## Life experiences

From a young age, I had health issues with asthma. I didn't know the Lord then. Over the years I have "gained" migraine, arthritis, back pain, shoulder problems, foot surgeries as well as the rape that happened to me, God was aware of all these. My back/spine problem for 23 years was very long time. God made me rest in those days. Even with my foot surgery I'm out of normal duties. Being on wheelchair, then crutches, and waiting for healing for 8 - 10 months, this has been a very long time. Nothing happened by coincidence, it's God's mighty plan for my life.

In  times like these, I'm able to be "still in God's presence" learning at His feet. I'm learning lessons for my own spiritual growth. I'm using  them to write my own experiences, how God's faithfulness never ceases. God is using me in writing books and tracts for outreach to our community.

Nursing School was great training place for me as a young Christian.  The believers in the Church I went to were great Christians. They blessed me with their lives.  God taught me to grow in His Word daily.  I learnt to live for Christ and shine for Him there.

I was able to gain knowledge about health as well as medical things for my whole life. I use it everywhere I go, in my home and also in nursing homes. I see God using me even when I was so new in my faith.

While at Gospel Schools, teaching many children about God was a great experience for me. I could freely meet with parents, share God's word also have Bible Studies with them. The studies I prepared to teach others whether to students, parents or Bible Study groups are still fresh in my mind.

Teaching children meant I had to learn much more from the Bible first. Where ever I teach today I still use it for serving Him.

When at the Bible School in Fiji, I enjoyed learning God's Word from godly teachers. God had also taught me to cook in large quantities. I used this skill to minister to children in the following years of ministry with all the camps and trips with the young people. We even ended up cooking at a big wedding as the cook didn't turn up. Only with prayer Vijay (one of our disciples from Fiji) and I got cooking for the guests. I couldn't cook for 300 people before. God blessed this food and everyone enjoyed the best food. It really was a great training ground for our ministry.

I learnt many things about city life at this time. God knew all the work I'll be involved in, school, churches, camps as well as in the community.  He prepared me fully to be equipped for the years that followed.

When I got married, all the new things I got involved in were incredible.  We visited people, shared the Gospel with Hindu families. We had Bible studies in homes as this brought great joy in our hearts. People needed practical help, whether it was in early morning or late at night, we were there for them. A pastor's job was always around the clock. Not many had transport. This was ministry for us as pastors.

Through Pat's life I learnt many things.  He was fully dedicated to put God first in his life. He was a man of integrity, passion for God and compassion for people. He was a great teacher of God's Word.

When we arrived into Australia, it was really strange. Our family experienced the love of Christ first hand. People like Tanga, Vijay, Uncle Allan, Aunty Saroj, Rajen, Cynthia, Pradeep, Vijen, Madhu and many others, provided us with everything we needed in our home. Some of these people we had never met before. In Christ they did a great job to make us comfortable. We settled in very quickly. We praise God for their generosity and love shown to us when we needed it most. Thank you!

I learnt from these lovely people that I could either be a wonderful godly person or be selfish being. They gave us all they could. I learnt to be selfless, giving to others especially those who came from other countries as students or migrants.  I have done my best to be of assistance to others in the same way as I was treated.

I really wanted to graduate at Emmaus Bible College but God put me aside for a purpose. I put in all my effort in studies but I still couldn't make it as my arthritis played up badly. I continued doing simple things like being hospitable, serving needy people as this was a great need.

Many students were hurting.  God used me to care for them as my own children rather than thinking of my studies. Being there to listen to them, pray with them, did not need any degrees or qualifications.  These gifts I can use today and always, in Myanmar, Fiji, India, Australia or any part of the world. These are the talents God has given me so I can always use them for His glory.

After Pat was called home, my life was extremely difficult.  My father's words came to my mind " you love each other too much, you two should separate yourselves a bit, what will happen if one of you should be taken away, it will be very hard for the other to live" that's exactly true.  How hard? I didn't know then! This was true wisdom from my dad. I know now the toughest kind of suffering!

The worst tragedy anyone could go through is death of a spouse. How can we undo the things we have learnt to do over all those many years.  We can't stop when God calls us home. I don't wish for anyone to die but I can understand how difficult it is to go through this situation.

**Blessings and more**

Even when I didn't know I was having a second surgery, God provided a home for me with lifts. This home has every convenience needed for my recovery time.

This home really was a miracle to us. Many people applied for this home but God gave it to us.  As we saw many people viewing this place, Reg was worried we will not get this place.  I said Reg "let's pray together that God will give this house to us" I really believed that God will do miracles. I even told Aaron I had given the notice to my other place. He said to me "Mum why would you do that, you don't know if you will get this place"

Two days after, I heard from the Real Estate to say I got the place. I thanked God for this. I called Regi, I had to tell him over and over, "it is true God heard our prayers" Aaron didn't believe either. One thing Aaron always tells me "Mum, you seem to have a direct line with God." Well, I am no different from others, a  sinner saved by God's grace. I just praise God He hears our prayers. Surely when God opens the door, nobody can close it. These things bring us closer to God who is able to do for us what no one else can do.

Kushma, children and grandson Zac, 2011

Kushma and Joni Eareckson Tada: meeting up with the woman of my dreams! Olympics, 2000

Celebrating mum's 76th Birthday and permanent residency, January 2012

Why do people think there is no God? How can we say we don't need God? I couldn't do anything if God was not in my life. With him, all things have been possible—my grandson, my children's education, their weddings, their jobs, the right partners, all was done by God Himself. These were very important aspects of their lives. Where would I have gone to find the right person for them? But God in His wisdom did this. For Hazel and Aaron to have a baby was important. God made sure they trusted in Him more than the doctors, He knew in His wisdom the right timing. He provided them with this miracle. His timing was absolutely perfect, Nigel's wedding, my surgery, Hazel's baby, my new home and then my second surgery. The list goes on and on. All of life's puzzle He puts into the right place.

In those days, when in lots of pain, time was very slow as day after day I could feel the pain lingering. The day seemed too long. Today I feel the joy in my heart of "How Great Is Our God!" When I look back at the things we as a family endured, how one by one God in His strength and power, He enabled us to carry on. I give glory to God for His outstanding work done in us. We rejoice in the Lord as we count our blessings one by one. Thank you Lord for all you have taught me in my life!

Why should I complain? Look at all those suffering in nursing homes and hospitals. We all have problems. Not all of us go through the same things in life. I know God chose me to lose my husband. My suffering maybe different to my friends, but we are all important to the Lord. He cares for all our different needs. To reiterate the verse I have mentioned earlier, **1 Corintians 10:13 "Every test that you have experienced is the kind that normally comes to people. But God keeps his promise, and he will not allow you to be tested beyond your power to remain firm; at the time you are put to the test, he will give you the strength to endure it, and so provide you with a way out."**

I think my friend would have been in more pain all her life than me. From the days together in Fiji, we have prayed for each other.

My friend from thirty six years ago, and I have seen each other's difficulties. We have prayed many prayers. Her trials are totally different from mine. Does that mean it's not hard for her? Of course not! Everyone of our trials may come in different ways. I think she would have been in more pain all her life than I have been. From our days together in Fiji, we have prayed for each other. We helped each other through all the difficulties. Her problems were totally different from mine. God graciously used me to help her along those days to build her in her spiritual life. Like me, once her spiritual life got on the right track, all other things fell in the right place too. Mathew 6:33 Seek first God's kingdom and all other things will be added to you. When problems got worse in her life, she didn't know how to handle things. If God is not in our lives we can't handle any problems at all. Like me she also thought God had abandoned her. I have tried my best to be of help to her throughout our friendship.

Today, I see a different person in her altogether. She has truly grown stronger through all these trials she has faced. Many problems haven't gone away but our God gives us strength to take one day at a time praying for these things even now. We have prayed for many little things throughout. God brought the answers in the right time. In the last ten years, she has grown a great deal spiritually. She knows scripture and quotes them to me throughout our conversations. We love each other dearly. She has cared for me like a little sister would have done. When I was in difficulties she surely was there for me all the way. God is using my dear friend today to encourage me and countless others as she serves God. Praise God for wonderful close friends!

"When good things come to our lives, we are just so happy and excited to accept them. Why should we complain when it's time for us to suffer?" said Dr James.  We are sharing in the suffering of Christ when we go through all these problems as well as sickness. God really opened my eyes.  My Lord suffered so much pain, brutality, mocking and beating, what is my little pain in comparison? When I think of this, I feel ashamed to even compare my life with the King of Kings and the Lord of Lords.  What a blessing to belong to this King and Master!

Last year in March, after my first surgery I started writing this book. I could not concentrate and finish this.  Lots of things came my way. I loved caring for my little grandson for two days a week. This was the most relaxing time I had. My mum needed a lot of attention as she wasn't well. She had many health issues to deal with. She ended up having a surgery as I continued to care for her. Those many trips I took mum to doctors, immigration, Medicare, hospitals were all learning process for me as well. While mum was with us we as a family decided to get her Permanent Residence for this country. I guess you know how much paper work is involved in this.

My dear mum got her Australian Permanent Residence Visa on her birthday in January.  I am grateful to God for honouring my mum in a very special way. Mum has been a great mum in caring for us all our lives. These things were just tiny things I could do in return. Unfortunately, the pressure was too much for my foot and one of the screws broke while I was running errands for my family.

My brother Rajen and sister Nalesh did a great job taking care of mum, while I went into hospital for the second surgery. Praise God, my mum is in good health now, enjoying with her other children in New Zealand. My children took care of me in my difficult healing process. Regi really surprised me in the amount of work he did before he went to work.  I praise God for my children who did all they could to make me very comfortable.

"Time is the best thing you can give to anyone"

We all, whether it's my mum, nursing home resident or anyone, everyone just wants a little time, a little love from us. Our world is hurting, so broken, searching for love. If only we could do a little everyday to show that love of God to someone, many more people would come into God's Kingdom.

Over the years in every difficult situation, first I ran to tell others, one after another. I know none of them could help me through my trials and difficulties.  Only God could do the job really well. I feel ashamed how many times I let my God down. Yet He has continued to forgive me.

Now I run to God.  As I have been studying, I put my name is the verses of the Bible.  It has really made sense to me, how intimate is my God.
Isaiah 40:10

Kushma, **"I am the Lord your God, I am holding your right hand and I tell you, don't be afraid, I will help you."**

Psalm 32: 8 The Lord says **"I will make you wise** (Kushma). **I will show you where to go. I will guide you and watch over you."**

**God's complete knowledge and care (for me)**
Psalm 139: 13, 15, 16

**You (GOD) created every part of me; you put me together in my mother's womb. When my bones were being formed, carefully put together in my mother's womb, when I was growing there in secret, You (GOD) knew I was there. You (God) saw me before I was born. The days allotted to me had all been recorded in your book, before any of them ever began.**

This is God's way of teaching and training me now. Study and meditate on His word first. Then be sure to do everything He says through His word. God guides me as I take one day at a time in my life. He hasn't finished with me yet. God is working in my life every day. He has His eyes on me 365 days of the year, twenty-four hours a day, every minute and every second. My life is like a construction site: "WORK IN PROGRESS"

I enjoy loving Him, talking to Him and sharing my pain and all my gain. I thank Him. Now that I have been alone for all these years, when no one wants to listen to me, I'm fine God is never tired of listening to me. When my husband passed away my boys told me, "You should get married again, mum." I asked why, they told me I talk too much! "At least someone will listen to you" I'm happy God never gets tired of listening to me.

I had so many questions in my life as you may have read. All the answers to my life's problems are in the Bible. I was even scared "what if there is no heaven." As I searched the Scriptures, I found out many places in the Bible about heaven.

In Revelation, I have learnt that Heaven is a wonderful place; there is no more sorrows, pain, no death, or crying how wonderful will this be when I get there! I will see my husband and all my loved ones too.

**In John 14:1-6**
 **When Jesus said "I am going to prepare a place for you.....so that where I am there you will be also. Jesus said that I am the WAY, the TRUTH and the LIFE, no man goes to the Father (in Heaven) except through me"**

**John 3:16 (NIV)**
**For God so loved the world (all the people of the world) that He gave His one and only son, (Jesus) that whoever (like you and me) believes in Him shall not perish but have Eternal life (in Heaven)**

Do you know for sure where you will spend Eternity?  The Bible is the only book that is not out of date.  This has been there for centuries and will be there forever. This is not only a book but the words speak to our hearts changing lives forever. Bible tells us there is Heaven and Hell. I know I am on my way to Heaven. Jesus died for all my sins. I have accepted the truth that Jesus is one who died for all my sins past, present and future sins. If I believe in Him I become his child.

**John 1:12 tells us "As many as received Him, to them gave He the right to become children of God".**

At any funeral people talk about the lovely things you have done in life. What about your soul? Are you sure you are going to Heaven? Are you ready to meet God? If you have any doubt please give your life to Jesus who died for you on the cross. Give your heart to Him. Trust in Him. Confess all your sins to Him. He will forgive you for all your wrongs.  Accept Him as your God and Saviour. You will also become a child of God. You will be ready to meet him in Heaven. Say this little prayer to Jesus with all your heart:

"Dear Lord Jesus I know I am a sinner. I have done many wrong things in my life. I know you died for all my sins on that Cross. Please forgive me of all my sins. Clean my heart and come into my life, I want to live for you all my life. In Jesus Name Amen"

This is when you become a child of God. To get more help you can start reading from the book of John in the Bible. This will help you grow in Christ. If you don't have a Bible ring or see your nearest Church Pastor for help.  You will find lots of words in the Bible that will encourage you every day.  It is my prayer that your life will be blessed by God as you walk in the Truth of His Word.  If you need more information please email me on: lifeinitsfullness@ gmail.com

Our life is a gift from God. He has given us everything in life, our family, our jobs, our homes and all that we have. Sometimes we think "when I get older I will do things for God." Before you know it, your life will be gone, like my husband's. We don't know if we have another month or a year ahead of us. Accidents happen. Cancer kills us. How would you feel if something like this shortens your life? Let us all live to please God.  "Only what we do for God will last for eternity."  Can I encourage you to live every day like this is your last day. Let's do our very best for our Mighty God. When I face him in Heaven, I'd like to hear, "Well done, good and faithful servant!"

God has His hands on me every day. He will do the same for you too. He will guide you in your life. Remember every experience that is painful to go through will build your character as it did mine. Experience is the best teacher.

When **"We love God with all your heart, with all your soul, and with all your strength with all your mind; and love your neighbour as we love ourselves,"** we have done well Luke 10:27

Think of this:

When we get to Heaven we will be asked some things and what will our answer be?

# The Choice is yours:

God won't ask what kind of car you drove but He will ask how many you drove who needed help

God won't ask how big your house is but He will ask how many people you welcomed into your home

God won't ask about the clothes in your closet but He will ask how many you helped to clothe

God won't ask how many material possessions you had but He will ask if they dictated your life

God won't ask what your highest salary was but He will ask if you compromised your character to obtain it

God won't ask how many promotions you received but He will ask how you promoted others.

God won't ask what your job title was, He will ask if you performed your job to the best of your ability

God won't ask how many friends you had, He will ask how many people to whom you were a friend

God won't ask in what neighbourhood you lived, He will ask how you treated your neighbours

Taken from (CBMC International, Monday Manna, March 2002)

# References

"The choice is yours," CBMC International, Monday Manna, March 2002

"Jesus you are my firm foundation," Words & Music ©1994 Integrity's Hosanna Music/ Integrity Praise, administered by Kingsway's Thank you Music, PO Box 75  Eastbourne, East Sussex BN23 6NW, UK

"Because He lives I can face tomorrow," Copyright 2012 written by Bill & Gloria Gaither, Produced by: David Crowder, Executive producer: Louie Giglio, Shelly Giglio, and Brad O Donnel.
Worshiptogether.com Songs/ sixteps Music ASCAP, Admin at EMICMPGPublishing.com

An Indian Song: "Aaj ki raat eh kaisi raat" Aman 1967  Artist Saira Banu,

Count Your Blessings, Johnson Oatman, Jr.
Publication 1897 © Copyright Public Domain

Scriptures cited in: The Everyday Bible, New Century Version © 1987 by Worthy Publishing, Fort Worth, Texas, 76137. Used by permission.

Scripture cited in the Holy Bible, New International Version®, NIV® copyright © 1973, 1978, 1984, 2011 by Biblica, Inc™ used by permission

Scripture cited in Good News Bible (UK/British edition) British & Foreign Bible Society